The Family Freedom Project

A step-by-step guide to living
abroad with kids.
From dream to plan to reality.

By Liisa Vexler

Dedication

To Derek. You give us this life of love and laughter.

To Dexter and Charlie, who taught me to once again question, to wonder and to see the joy in every moment.

Contents

Preface

Open your eyes, look within. Are you satisfied with the life you're living?

Bob Marley

Before we get into our story, I want to tell you what this book is not. This is not a story about overworked urbanites who make a break from it all, sell all their possessions and live on very little in a tropical paradise. This is not a travel guide, though you may find references to easily replicable adventures that you might enjoy with your loved ones, both in this book and on The Family Freedom Project blog. Most importantly, this is not a story about retirement in any way, shape or form.

What you are about to read is the story of one family that loves freedom and adventure; a family that values time and experience above all else - life is short after all. This is the story of a family that decided to move away from convention and design a life that allows the freedom and flexibility to enjoy every meaningful moment.

My friends and family inspired this book. It was also inspired by all the strangers who contacted me through online forums asking me questions about how we live the way we do. It is intended to be an entertaining and personal read that will demystify the steps we took to get where we are today; I am writing on a balcony overlooking the main street of Tamarindo, Costa Rica.

Along the way, you will read about our struggles and our successes. You will pick up amazing travel tips and learn how to get less (or no) paper mail, get rid of your excess "stuff" and streamline life so it's easier to focus on the aspects that are important to you.

Whether or not you want to travel with your family, live abroad with your family, or simply de-clutter your life, I believe that this book has something in it for you.

How to Use This Guide

A man who dares to waste one hour of time has not discovered the value of life.

Charles Darwin

We believe we live our life by our own design, purposefully shaped and molded to fit our needs and desires. Family, friends, peers and society all contribute to the expectations we set for our lives, but it is important to be true to our own needs first and foremost. By acknowledging the expectations of others, but following the path that we choose, we find meaning and joy in everyday life.

While I could have written this as a story about personal family travel and adventure or as a travelogue, I chose instead to weave our experiences into a useful tool that can help others live the life they design for themselves and their families.

Snapshots of our journey are incorporated into this guide, along with a formula that I have developed to help others break away from the same restrictions our family works hard to avoid. This is a guide designed to help you free yourself and your family from geographical boundaries or time restrictions – a handbook to working and living where you want, when you want.

Though this is a how-to for families with children who want to learn more about living abroad, it is my belief that this book is for everyone. If you are part of a family looking to shift your lifestyle, then you have discovered a tool that will help you get there. If you are simply curious about how others live their lives, this book is also for you. You may glean tidbits that you can use in your life, or you may simply read for interest - both approaches and outcomes are suitable.

If you truly want to make a move with your family, I recommend reading the book from start to finish, and then returning to the how-to sections and checklists to digest them in more detail. These are the tools that will be most useful for you on your journey.

The book format is a manual for travel abroad with kids, blended with our family's story, interspersed with practical notes. I hate to call these notes "advice," but maybe they are advice – useful step-by-step tools coupled with amusing anecdotes about daily life and travel.

My hope is that this book will be a catalyst, that it will take you from "dreamer" mode to well on your way with a plan of action.

If there is one message that I hope you take from my writing, it is this: Get started today. Don't wait. Life is short. Turn your dream into a plan, and make it a reality.

Finally, this guide is part of a larger conversation and shift in the way families live, work and think today. I love hearing from readers and answer all my mail myself. I hope you will <u>join the conversation</u>.

Welcome to The Family Freedom Project!

Part 1: Seeing the Possibilities

And whenever I'd complain or was upset about something in my own life, my mother had the same advice: "Darling, just change the channel. You are in control of the clicker. Don't replay the bad, scary movie."

Arianna Huffington

Raised by professional, one-place/one-career parents, my husband and I both expected to complete post-secondary educations and go on to have professions of our own. When neither of us found passion in higher learning, we embarked on our own journeys. I won't speak for my husband, Derek, but I know I had misgivings about not sticking with one career. Why couldn't I stay in a job for more than a few years while my friends moved up the corporate or professional ladder?

When Derek and I became a couple, I realized from him that my passion lay in life itself, experiencing all that it had to offer, without making work my sole focus. His entrepreneurial spirit ignited my own, and together we realized the possibilities for our future together.

Our Story

The purpose of our lives is to be happy.

Dalai Lama

Almost daily, a tourist will ask me how long I have been in Tamarindo and where I am from originally. They will then ask half a dozen questions about how I have come to live the life I do. Before I describe what that life involves, I want to give you the succinct answer to the "how do you do that?" question.

It's simple: Derek and I are self-employed and both work online. I am a freelance writer primarily in the health and medical fields and Derek is the proprietor of a network of job search websites. While many of our friends in Costa Rica have arrived here in different ways, the simplest, fastest way to live a life free of geographical restrictions or accountability to someone else for your time is to work online for yourself.

But how and why did we get here? And can you do it too?

Hint: The answer is a resounding "Yes" to the second question!

Before we break down the process so you can see just how straightforward it can be, let's dive into our story so you have some context.

A Family History of Travel

In my medical writing work, I often write about genetic risk factors. *The patient has a family history of heart disease*, I will write, or *family history is negative for cancer.* If travel were a medical condition, I would definitely have the travel bug, passed on through maternal genes and spread through contact to my paternal side.

I come from parents who love to travel. These days, with my dad in semi-retirement, my parents travel on average a week out of every month. In any given year they will ski in the American Rockies, cycle in Italy or trek across a glacier in southern Chile.

My brother has this genetic condition as well. He and his family live in London, England. We all meet every year or two for a family vacation near one of our respective homes.

It has always been this way, though travel was less frequent and less exotic when my brother and I were young.

In 1975, my parents packed me up and took me to Lyon, France, where my dad spent a year learning French and pursuing a cardiology fellowship in a language he was just learning. In those days, my parents sent audiotapes and letters back and forth to my grandparents in Canada to keep them connected to their 2-year-old grandchild (me!).

If taking a young child across the world in the mid-70s could be done, then with today's ubiquitous high-speed communication and air travel, I knew that packing up our family to live abroad could be easily achieved.

Though my family only lived in France for a year, it was an important one. If our family history were written, that period in France would take up a lot of space in that book. My brother may disagree, since he was not yet born, but it was a significant time for my parents, and I believe it was also a defining time for me. I knew from the very beginning of my life that borders were made for crossing, languages for learning, and adventure and change were something to seek in life.

Falling In Love With A New Country

Five months into our marriage, Derek and I embarked on a delayed three-week honeymoon in Costa Rica. We had hoped to go to Italy, but the Euro was so strong in 2004 that a three-week trip was cost-prohibitive. Costa Rica was relatively cheap in comparison, and almost equally appealing. What it lacked in gastronomy and history, it made up for in natural splendor.

We planned to stay in four destinations around the country. We would touch down in San Jose and stay the night, then travel to the Arenal volcano area for a couple of days and move on to Tamarindo, described in the guidebooks as a surf town on the Pacific northwest coast with gorgeous beaches.

Tamarindo Feels Like Home

By the third day of our four-day stay in Tamarindo, we had developed a daily routine:

Up at the crack of dawn to the deep growls of the howler monkeys, we would try fruitlessly to get back to sleep. Eventually, I would pull on my favorite bathing suit and Derek would find a pair of dry shorts so we could head out to for the day.

First on the agenda was a leisurely breakfast overlooking the ocean, watching the resident magpie jays trying to steal the packets of sugar from the restaurant tables.

Eventually, as I finished my third cup of fragrant Costa Rican coffee, we would think about what the rest of the day had in store for us. But first, a walk on the beach.

Tamarindo beach is about 2.25 km from end to end, a walk that took us about 45 minutes at a leisurely pace.

We would walk and we would talk, contemplating life and, as most newlyweds do, imagining what our future together would hold.

"Could you imagine living in a place like this?" Derek asked one day.

I could. More than imagining it, I could envision it.

I envisioned us living outside our native Canada in a country where we could learn the language and absorb a new culture. I had studied Spanish for a year in university. I understood the rudiments and could place an order in a restaurant or make a purchase in a shop - no more, no less.

We continued to walk and to talk, discussing the possibilities but making no plans. It was too early to uproot, but we had planted the first seed of radical change.

On our return home to Canada we told everyone who would listen about what a great trip we had had. Our good friend Mike challenged us to rate the trip on a scale of one to ten. "A ten," we both exclaimed simultaneously.

"Will you go back?" he asked.

"Someday," we replied.

Mike continued to probe: Why wouldn't we take our next vacation in Costa Rica if we rated it so highly?

One of us, I cannot remember who, told him that we had other places to see. In honest hindsight, I think we wanted to preserve the joyous memory of our stay in Costa Rica, rather than risk any disappointment by returning too soon.

Returning to Costa Rica

Almost five years after our enchanting honeymoon, we considered a return to Costa Rica. Since our last visit, we had welcomed two children into our family. Dexter was now 3 ½ and Charlie was 18 months. We had been on several family vacations with the boys, but we had not been back to Costa Rica.

In March 2009, my parents eagerly agreed to take care of the boys for a week while Derek and I spent some time resting and recharging.

It was time to go back to Costa Rica.

We made reservations at the same hotel we had stayed at five years earlier, Hotel Capitan Suizo in Tamarindo. We planned seven nights of peace and seven days of sun, surf and sand.

Costa Rica didn't disappoint.

On day four we visited several rental properties with a local real estate agent. On day five we made a visit to the closest bilingual preschool to Tamarindo.

The seed we planted on our last trip had now sprouted, and it was beginning to grow roots.

My Facebook account, a useful source of recent personal history, reminds me of what I thought of that trip. In response to a "how was your trip?" message from a friend, I replied:

Trip was awesome - fantastic weather, great food, lovely people - everything we expected!

Will the Kids Like It Too?

Less than a year later, we traveled back to Tamarindo with the kids, renting a condo across the street from our favorite hotel. Two-year-old Charlie and four-year-old Dexter loved it immediately. They enjoyed visiting the orphan howler monkeys at Hotel Capitan Suizo, they loved watching the iguanas poop, and most of all, they could not get enough of the sun, the sand, and the water.

A two-week trip to a single destination is sufficiently long for you to develop a daily routine. We would wake up to the growls of the howler monkeys, eat a light breakfast - oh, Costa Rican coffee, how I love thee - and pack up the kids for the beach.

Derek would always work for a little while before we left the house, while the boys and I would play outside in the pool.

Derek does not take a day off work - EVER. He may not work long hours, but he must check in via his computer daily. He does not believe that an extra 30 minutes of leisure time is worth the potential loss in revenue if he misses a technical problem that could have easily been fixed. For this reason, we rarely travel for extended periods anywhere that does not have a high-speed Internet connection. In a hotel, WiFi access in the lobby or restaurant is sufficient, but Derek insists on some sort of access.

Derek's refusal to take a full 24 hours off used to bother me, but not anymore, not when we can travel for weeks at a time, or Derek can take any given afternoon off with no hesitation. He coaches the boys' sports, never misses a game because of work, and can attend all of their parent-teacher conferences.

On Vacation in Tamarindo with Preschoolers

Tamarindo beach is vast, and down at the far south end where we were staying, there is hardly ever more than one or two other couples or groups around. The boys made roads in the sand while I tried unsuccessfully to read, being called upon often to assist with the roadwork.

Midday, we would walk the seven minutes along the beach into the center of town. Our favorite lunch spot was the Italian deli for pizza and salads. The boys drank *batidos* (smoothies pronounced ba-tee-dos) almost every day, sometimes twice a day. In Costa Rica smoothies are made from your choice of fruit, your choice of water or milk, and sugar - a couple of teaspoons of sugar per smoothie.

When we got home to Canada after this vacation, I noticed that Dexter had developed some seriously chubby cheeks. Sugary smoothies every day can affect even the most active among us. I put him on a secret diet for a week, feeding him all-he-could-eat broccoli and chicken, apple and chickpeas, among other similar choices. He was none the wiser, and his cheeks deflated to their regular 4-year-old cuteness in no time.

My parents joined us for part of that vacation. They arrived a couple of days after we did, having spent a few days trekking through the cloud forests of Monteverde. We had a great time at the beach and the pool with them. My mom and dad like action, activity and sightseeing. We decided that though our kids were small, we could manage a two-hour tour through the estuary. It was a total success and this is a tour I recommend to all families with young children or other mobility-challenged visitors.

After about five days, my mom and dad returned to Canada and we spent a second week at the beach. We must have eaten at all the restaurants in town. My idea of a vacation does not include cooking, and thus on vacation we rarely eat at home. Tamarindo has between 50 and 60 restaurants at any given time, with 5,000 people living in the town during the dry season, which means that there is one restaurant for every 100 people. For this reason, many restaurants don't survive, but there are some that do, usually because they are consistently great.

A friend from Wisconsin recently commented to me that Tamarindo is full of culture compared to where she comes from in the American Midwest. "In which other small town she asked, "can you get falafel made by Israelis, pizza and gelato made by Italians, steak prepared by Argentinians, not to mention the ceviche, tacos, and other local Costa Rican specialties available here?"

How right she was.

At the end of our two-week vacation, I was glad to go home. I found the last few days a little boring; I had had my fill of building roads through the sand into the Pacific.

I told Derek very clearly that next time - and that there would be a next time was understood - I would prefer to return for at least a month and take Spanish classes. "More like two months," Derek suggested, "That way the kids can go to school."

"Yes," I replied. Two months sounded about right. Our plan was starting to take shape.

Defining Happiness

I am never bored; to be bored is an insult to one's self.

Jules Renard

Let's begin breaking down our plan with a simple question that has an illuminating answer.

What is the Opposite of Happiness?

Is it sadness?

Nope. That's not it.

Just as love's opposite is not the equally passion-filled emotion of hate, but rather impassionate indifference, the opposite of happiness is not sadness.

Boredom is the opposite of happiness.

Are You Happy?

A multitude of self-help books and articles have been written about finding happiness. If you are asking yourself if you are happy on a regular basis, you probably are not.

You are probably bored.

Through my journey as a parent, I have learned that the excitement in my life, the ups, the downs, the great successes and tear-inducing utter failures, are all part of my joy and happiness – because I am NEVER bored.

We have experienced major challenges in business and with our children. We have had amazing successes in these realms as well. We have travelled as tourists and lived as expats. We have laughed and we have cried. Our less-conventional life, though so conventional compared to some families we have met over the past couple of years, keeps us fulfilled, excited and happy.

When you consider your happiness, think about how you keep your life from becoming or being boring.

What I Find Boring Might Be Thrilling for You

Though I do believe that happiness stems from the absence of boredom, I do not believe that you must travel or bounce from crisis to crisis to be happy. Different factors stimulate each of us as individuals.

I have a friend whose fourth child turned one this week. She does not travel far nor do I see her daily routine changing on a regular basis. However, she exudes joy. Her children bring her the diversion and challenge that allow her to never be bored and thus to be happy.

Exercise

Ask yourself: What makes me happy today?

List 3 or 4 things that fill your life with emotion today

1._____

2. _____

3. _____

An example of my answers on one particular day:

1. I have a broken nose as a result of a surfboard and an errant wave at Playa Grande, Costa Rica.
2. I am writing about The Family Freedom Project right here today!
3. I finished another chapter of one of the books I am ghostwriting.
4. My children turned off their iPads without me having to beg or threaten.

If you find that you are in fact bored, read the following chapters with an eye to making a change. If you are happy -- maybe you are looking for something new or just plain curious -- go on reading too.

As you read, I want to make sure that you understand something: while our story makes our family who we are, we do not believe that ours is the only way to live. We thrive on risk and reward. Others do not. I do hope, though, that by reading about how we live, you may take a small step out of your comfort zone, whether consciously or unconsciously.

On the hanging bridges of the cloud forest in Monteverde, Dexter is far outside of his comfort zone and definitely not bored!

What is Lifestyle Design?

Focus on being productive instead of busy.

Timothy Ferriss

I wish I could pinpoint when we began to consciously define and design how we wanted to live, but I can't. It likely began before Derek and I were actually a couple, as both of us searched for something that would make our lives interesting and dynamic.

Derek has never had a "real job" beyond the time when he did four shifts bussing tables at a banquet hall in his teens. He has always been an entrepreneur.

Inspired by his freedom, success and lifestyle, I tried my hand, more or less successfully, at a couple of businesses. Never workaholics, we have always enjoyed our leisure time, and it was important for us to protect that, no matter how demanding the task at hand.

Marriage and children shifted our priorities even more. Now, protecting the time we had with each other and with our children was critical to our happiness. At the same time, we wanted to maintain our independent identities and, of course, ensure that our family had strong financial legs on which to stand.

While we have always enjoyed traveling, the idea of living abroad with the kids had not yet crystallized for us early in our relationship.

Yet, we still innately craved and valued experiences over goods or dollar signs, understanding that money was simply a means of creating experiences. Perhaps, we thought, if we made experience the goal of our pursuits rather than simply an intangible and ever-changing "financial stability," our choices would become clearer and our decisions easier to make.

So we did. We planned to move to Costa Rica for a first two-month trial adventure – which turned into a six-month trip once we began the planning. And, through many ups and downs that life has thrown at us since then, such as major business crises and a child whose quirks became more challenging, we have remained focused on the goal -- experience and family trump everything else.

Once this goal became clear to us, I became attracted to others with similar goals. I began reading books by authors who wrote from a similar perspective, and in Costa Rica I met many families and individuals with similar, or at least unique, views about the value of work and life's end game.

A few months before leaving for Costa Rica, in late 2011, a more formal lifestyle design plan began to take shape. I listened to Tim Ferriss' *4-Hour Work Week* on a friend's recommendation.

Day in and day out, I found myself retelling bits of Ferriss' story to Derek after long runs spent listening to the audiobook. What inspired me the most was that Tim was providing a framework for a process that we had already begun. We had already implemented much of what he suggested, but his book gave us even more tools and structure to prepare for our pursuits.

While Ferriss' book's lifestyle design model is specific and useful, only a very few will follow all of its principles to the letter. Some of his ideas are oversimplified and overly optimistic; others are not feasible for a family with children. His goals are based on the premise that everyone wants to live like the rich and famous, traveling the world looking for action and adventure. This simply isn't true. Individuals are fulfilled and motivated by different desires. However, his principles of lifestyle design, prioritizing and streamlining your life so you can spend time doing what you truly want to do, are sound. These were the catalyst that drove us further into our journey.

Implementing even a few of his suggestions or the suggestions I have for you later in the book can be life changing.

Lifestyle Design: What Is It?

Simply put, lifestyle design is precisely as its name suggests, the process of creating your own design and plan for your life.

You can start the process by asking yourself some simple, yet important (and sometimes difficult) questions:

1. What do you want to accomplish in your life?
2. What is important to you?
3. Where do you want to live? Make sure to consider your response to question 2 when answering this one.
4. How do you want to spend your time?

These are questions many of us never asked as we followed the expected path from high school to higher education and on to "a job."

The lifestyle design process makes you realize that you have choices in life. Though your parents may have strongly encouraged one path, you are the only one who chooses to stay in a job you hate or to keep paying the mortgage on that overly extravagant house.

When we start to dissect our path, we begin to understand that we - you, me, everyone - has complete control over all that we do. **If you don't like something in your life, you have the power to change it.** If you are where you want to be, keep on trucking, but even then, an understanding of the lifestyle design process may help you to live more deliberately and get even more of what you want.

Here are my answers to the above questions as an example. Yours will be different.

1. I have little need to accomplish anything in particular. I was born without major ambition, or perhaps an uncomplicated middle-class lifestyle nurtured it. I do hope to help where I can, see and experience as much as I can, and raise happy and healthy children. This sounds like a cliché, but so be it.

2. Family is my priority. Friends are a close second.

3. I want to live where it is warm, but I also want to live close to the people I love. For the most part, those I love live where it is cold -- really, really cold. I want to live in comfort. I don't like to rough it.

4. I want to spend my time being challenged, learning, doing, with friends and family around the world.

Once you have this basic understanding about what you want from life, you can then begin to design a lifestyle around your goals. But first, you must define your goals and make them slightly more concrete. I have three goals.

1. I want to be the one to accompany my kids to appointments, activities and school events.

2. I want to spend at least half the cold months of the winter where it is warm - Costa Rica is my second home these days.

3. I want to explore somewhere new a few times a year, sometimes with my kids, other times with my girlfriends, and often alone with my husband.

These are goals that can be revisited at any time. I could add work goals or personal development goals, but these three are the ones that guide how I structure and plan my life right now.

Ah yes, the plan. Planning is the key. You need to have a plan in order to reach your goals.

If you are not living the way you want to, this is your opportunity to create a plan to make it happen. Once you truly realize that you are the one in control of your life, you can start to enjoy the process of creating your ideal life.

Before we get to the nitty-gritty of planning, let's take a closer look at what lifestyle design can do for you and your family.

Why Design Your Life?

If you aren't yet convinced that purposeful lifestyle design is right for you, consider that lifestyle design is all about finding what suits you and your family. Instead of accepting the typical lifestyle that society and tradition have instructed you to follow, you determine your own path with your unique needs in mind.

Though all of our needs and wants are different, most people seek two simple, yet often elusive conditions: freedom and passion. Within these, everything is unique to your family - and it is all out there for the taking.

If you want to travel with your family or live abroad, then appropriate lifestyle design can make it happen. If you want to be the best stay-at-home mom possible, lifestyle design will also help. If you want more of that elusive work-life balance, lifestyle design will likely get you closer to that goal. The process is about defining what you want and taking steps to get there.

This process requires that you think only of your priorities and the needs of those who depend on you, your children or legal dependents. You cannot listen to what others may say about you or fear what they may think. Though it may sound selfish, this is about putting you and your family first.

Though some lifestyle changes are easy to implement, others are hard. In order to be successful, you must be passionate about the life you want to lead and dedicated to the plan you put in place. **No matter what type of lifestyle you envision, you need to be certain that the life you are moving toward is one you are passionate about living.**

If you are looking for a life of travel and adventure, and sell all your worldly possessions to move toward it, will you long for your morning ritual coffee in your favorite chair on your front porch? Do you sleep well in strange beds? Have you traveled before? Often we want what others have without understanding what it is that they have exactly.

Make sure your dream is really what you want, and not simply a reaction to what you do not want. You must be ready to accept everything that comes with your new lifestyle.

Why is it important to truly feel passionate about your lifestyle or the lifestyle you are working toward? Because the most important part of lifestyle design, especially the lifestyle design formula that we use in The Family Freedom Project, is freedom. If you are not passionate about your "why" for doing something, you will feel forced to do it, and then you are not truly free.

If you are passionate about the lifestyle you are working toward, you must next consider whether you are dedicated to making the changes required. Soon, we will begin to discuss how to make your plan, but it is important to know that no matter how feasible your plan, you will hit bumps along the road. We sure did.

We adapted and shifted some of the execution of our plan in order to maintain focus on the goal. When business was down, we cut spending. When our son was having trouble at school, we evaluated and took steps to make a change. These adjustments were not in the initial plan, but they kept us on the road (sometimes via a detour) to where we are going.

But wait!

I just said that we are still on the road to where we are going. Aren't we living our ultimate lifestyle? Yes, we are. But our ultimate goal is to keep moving forward on an exciting and adventurous, never-ending journey and thus we are still on the road, and will remain on it as long as we can.

On your journey, you will hit snags and bumps. You might get a bit bruised, but you will get up and get on with it, that is if you are passionate about the goal and dedicated to the process.

At this point, if you are still with me, you know where you want to go and you are passionate and dedicated to the idea. But how do you get there? You make a plan.

Part 2: Planning

A goal without a plan is just a wish.

Antoine de Saint-Exupéry

How do you change a dream into reality? You make a plan. Instead of thinking about taking your family abroad as something you will do somewhere down the line if all the stars align, you start thinking about it as something concrete – a reachable goal.

When Derek and I turned our dream into a plan, we put things in motion to get us there. Your plan may have a longer timeframe than ours, or it may be much shorter. Without timelines and clear objectives to work towards, though, your dream is just that—something intangible and unachievable.

Switch your thinking right now. Turn your dream into a plan.

Working to Live

Life is either a great adventure or nothing.

Helen Keller

I mentioned earlier in this book that Derek and I both work online for ourselves. Derek has job search websites. He makes revenue from pay-per-click advertising of jobs and other job-related products. He has been doing similar work since 2001.

I, on the other hand, have had a number of jobs and businesses over the past 15 years.

The businesses I started include:

- A tutoring service
- An event business for singles which I sold in 2004
- An online baby boutique which I liquidated in 2009

I was employed in various capacities as:

- A high school teacher
- A health research study manager/coordinator
- A public health communications manager
- Director of operations for a wholesale shopping website

When we began defining the goals for our family's lifestyle, we were quickly aware that if I wanted to work - and I did - I would have to find a way to find meaningful, challenging work online. I could not be accountable to someone else for my time if I wanted to be at every school function or medical appointment. This meant I needed to be not only working online but also self-employed. Finally, I would have to do something that did not require me to be available during traditional office hours.

What to do?

Without being limited by titles or degrees, I took stock of my skills and experience. I perused the Internet and peppered my friends in the healthcare and communications fields with questions, searching for employment ideas.

The best idea came from Derek. He uses a website called oDesk.com to hire freelance software developers for his websites. He suggested I take a look at the site to see if any freelance opportunities might suit my experience and expertise.

Medical transcription? Too low paying, and after the first week I would be bored. Medical billing? Same answer. Medical writing? Hmmm. I remembered that my friend Scott was a medical writer. I did some research and found various online certifications that might be useful as a medical writer, and I reached out to Scott for his input.

"Liisa," he said, "you don't need another qualification or certification to be a medical writer. You do it all the time as a research coordinator."

I did. I worked on manuscripts for peer-reviewed journals. I wrote marketing materials to attract patient participants for research studies. I could write for the consumer and for the scientist.

In that moment, in December 2012, I became: Liisa Vexler, Medical Writer.

On the advice of a friend who works in public relations with more than 100 employees under her, I did not use my resume to market myself. Instead, I created a professional bio highlighting all of my experience related to medical writing. It is my primary marketing piece, and it includes my photo.

Next, I signed up for <u>oDesk</u> and took a series of its tests that provide credibility to prospective clients. I created a website on <u>Weebly.com</u> in less than an hour. I made an appointment to have professional headshots taken. Within a week, I was up and running.

<u>oDesk.com</u> is a marketplace for freelance jobs. Freelancers, or contractors as they are called, are rated by clients and develop a reputation. Clients post projects and freelancers bid on them. There are jobs requiring all types of skills posted, and contractors of many levels to bid on them. At first, I was discouraged by the low rates that contractors from India, Bangladesh and the Philippines were bidding. I thought I would never be able to compete with them.

In order to develop a reputation, I began bidding on projects at a rate I deemed would garner me about $15 per hour. As my reputation grew over the first month or two, my rate doubled and has continued to grow significantly from there.

You do not have to be a writer to make this work. In fact, I would encourage you to try a different niche. Consider setting up a professional, high-quality virtual assistant business - and let me know because I might need your services. Or perhaps you are a whiz with Quickbooks. Why not set up a bookkeeping business? Are you familiar with specific online platforms such as Shopify or Wordpress? Market yourself as an expert and clients will come. I have noticed a growing number of ads for social media content providers online. If you love hanging out on Facebook or Twitter, this might be the right fit for you.

The first few assignments were nerve-wracking for me. Had I done a good job? Did my work measure up to "real" medical writers? I need not have worried. The feedback was unanimously positive. Some clients were more demanding than others, and I ended up firing those that were just too demanding, but the final outcome has been overwhelmingly positive.

If you do not have any skills or experience yet but want to make sure you remain free and mobile as you move forward in life, consider the following careers:

- Graphic designer
- Software programmer
- Bookkeeper
- Technical writer
- Translator
- Proofreader

I have primarily repeat clients and business from referrals now, and I have as much work as I want. The key to my success online comes, I believe, from clear communication with my clients. I always meet deadlines and deliver what we defined for the project. If you can do that, you will be doing more than 90% of online contractors already.

I work about 15 hours per week. I contribute to our family's bottom line, enough to cover all of our housing expenses, not just rent or mortgage. That is always the monthly goal. Most months I make more. If I wanted to work more, I could.

I believe that we could live abroad easily even if I was the sole breadwinner. It took me about a year to get to this point. During the first year I made enough to cover today's rent and utility expenses, still a respectable contribution to the household. If you want to work online and live off your income alone, I recommend giving yourself six months to a year to build up the business before embarking on your journey. That's plenty of time to get your housing situation in both your new and current locations organized if this is part of your plan, and get everything else planned out too.

Remember one truth as you prepare for your adventure:

It's mind-consuming, not time-consuming.

You can continue to work at your day job, take care of your kids and get an online business off the ground *if* you are organized and have a plan. If you are a risk-taker or have the means, you can go cold turkey and quit your day job to focus on what is most important to you now - the plan. Either way, it will be worth it in the end.

Freelance Marketplace Websites

oDesk.com is not the only online freelancer marketplace. Here are a few other multi-purpose ones that I have found. I know nothing about the quality of these, so do your own research to understand clearly how each one operates as it pays and protects its contractors.

Elance.com recently merged with oDesk but still separates platforms and sites.

Fiverr.com only pays $5 per task, hence the name, but you can add additional services for more than the basic $5 service you offer.

More freelancer marketplace websites:

    Guru.com
    Peopleperhour.com
    iFreelance.com
    Sologig.com
    Hour.ly

Your Challenge

Dig up the job description for the position you currently have. If none exists, create one. Do the same for your most recent previous positions. Then, list skills that you could use as a freelancer. It does not matter if they were not the primary focus of your job. If you can do them, they count.

Investigate the market for freelancers with the skills and experience that you have. Spend a lot of time perusing the categories on some of the websites listed above. Pick one or two that could become your specialty.

Then, write your bio. Feel free to use the template I have provided below, or get creative. You can then repurpose this bio for use on your personal website. I consider a website a must because it establishes your legitimacy as a professional.

Professional Bio Template

A Passion for [ ] and [ ]

[YOUR FIRST AND LAST NAME] is a [YOUR NEW SPECIALTY] with [x] years experience in the [GENERAL] field.

[YOUR FIRST NAME]'s skill set includes an ability to [3 SKILLS NECESSARY FOR THE JOB]. He/She has experience in [A MINIMUM OF 3, UP TO A MAXIMUM OF 6 TASKS RELATED TO THE WORK] as well as [ONE MORE SKILL]. [YOUR FIRST NAME] believes that [SOMETHING CRITICAL TO DOING THE JOB SUCCESSFULLY, i.e., storytelling for writers]

[YOUR FIRST NAME] began his/her career in [give year], spending [TIME PERIOD] working at [RELATED JOB]. [YOUR FIRST NAME]'s passion for [SKILL YOU ACQUIRED AND WILL USE IN SPECIALTY] was born here, and he/she [SOMETHING YOU DID WITH THAT SKILL].

[A LINE ABOUT ANOTHER RELATED POSITION AND SOMETHING YOU LEARNED THERE].

Most recently, [FIRST NAME] worked at the [NAME OF EMPLOYER] as the [TITLE AND ANY PARTICULARLY IMPRESSIVE RESPONSIBILITIES].

[YOUR FIRST NAME] graduated from [FIRST DEGREE OR CERTIFICATE] with a [NAME OF DEGREE OR CERTIFICATE]. He/She went on to [OTHER RELEVANT TRAINING].

[YOUR EMAIL]

[YOUR WEBSITE URL]

*NB I have not included a phone number on my profile. This is deliberate. You are going to move away from using telephone communication as much as possible as you move through the chapters.

Now go to it. Leverage your skills to create the online, mobile, flexible career you want. Work when you want, where you want, for only yourself and your family.

Overcoming Obstacles

There is no illusion greater than fear.

Lao Tzu

In order to achieve your goal, you need to break down the barriers that are standing in your way. And there are always barriers. However, few barriers are insurmountable; they may just need time, patience and often a giant leap of faith to get you over them, around them, or blasting right through them.

The first step to overcoming obstacles will be to identify them - all of them. Is fear holding you back? Are your responsibilities at home or at work impossible to escape? Or, is it financial concerns that are keeping your from putting your plan into action?

Obstacles come in all forms, shapes and sizes, but almost all of those that I have heard someone bring up can be categorized into three groups:

1. Emotional barriers
2. Financial barriers
3. Logistical barriers

Let's define each group of barriers to understand where each of your obstacles fits so that you can address it as it comes up.

Emotional Barriers

Emotional barriers are intangible sentiments that are keeping you from putting a plan into action. Fear is by far the number one emotion that prevents individuals from moving forward on any big life change. Fear is the emotion that causes us to ask questions that begin with "What if"?

What if I don't like it?

What if we get sick?

What if something happens to a loved one back home?

I have asked myself these "what if" questions and hundreds more. I come from a family of worriers; anxiety is in my DNA. I know that I cannot avoid the questions, so I ask them, but it is what I do with these questions and their answers that allows me to overcome this potential obstacle.

Other emotions that may hold you back are uncertainty, frustration or anger. How can each of these emotions hold you back? Simply put, you may be committing too much energy to these emotions.

Each of us has a finite amount of energy. From that pool of energy, we pull out "units" to spend on mental, physical and emotional tasks throughout our day. If you are allotting all of your energy to feeling angry, you may have little mental, emotional or even physical energy left to put any type of plan into motion, let alone one that requires a complete change in lifestyle.

Am I saying you can't ever be angry or frustrated? Of course not! I am just suggesting that if these emotions are taking up space in your psyche, they may be draining you and possibly have created an obstacle that is preventing you from moving forward on your plan.

I am not a health professional, so I cannot give you advice on how to move away from dwelling on certain emotions, but I can tell you what I do when I feel fear or uncertainty blocking my path; I allow myself to indulge in those emotions. I take the "what if's" to their very end - you know, like the plane crashes. Then I ask myself if at that ultimate end I would be happy with all the decisions I had made up to that point. If I won't be, I go back to my hypothetical chain of events and change the plan. When you give a name to your ultimate fears or frustrations, they become less daunting, more tangible, and easier to address.

There have been many books written on the topic of emotional stagnancy. This is not one of them. Just understand, if you are being held back by an emotional fear (or two), you do have the power to overcome this daunting, yet NOT insurmountable obstacle.

Financial Barriers

This is by far the most commonly cited reason why people feel they cannot take their families away from their current home and/or life. There is no doubt that this can be a challenging piece of the puzzle, but it is by no means a barrier that cannot be pushed out of the way. We all live on different budgets in our home countries, so there is no reason that you should expect to live abroad or even at home in the same way that your neighbor does.

Family travel, family life abroad and even family life at home can be lived on a shoestring or on a big budget. It is a matter of making choices and planning for all eventualities. Ask any personal financial expert and they will be unanimous in their advice: If you truly want to make a change and provide new experiences for yourself and your family, you will need to make a financial plan.

The intricacies of your financial plan will be unique to your current situation. If you have been saving for a splurge vacation and are currently self-employed, you may be closer to your goal than someone who works in the service industry and spends all of his pay cheques each month. While one person may be closer to the goal than the other, both can get there with proper tools and planning.

A little later in this book we will look at specific tools you can use to help with financial planning. In this chapter I will simply list the five ways that you can make geographic freedom possible without worry about finances. If you can fit into one of these categories, you can make it happen:

- You are independently wealthy thanks to a recent lottery win, large inheritance or the lucrative sale of your Internet start-up.

- You are able to convince your employer that you can work remotely.

- You are self-employed or become a freelancer.

- Your employer provides an income-averaging opportunity, allowing you to take 80% of your salary for four years and then take the fifth year off while your job is held and you are paid, or other similar structure.

- You save your money until you feel that you have enough for what you are planning.

Where do you see yourself fitting into the above? Do not allow negative thoughts to creep in at this point. It may be scary to consider the possibilities, but you cannot ignore that they exist and one more of your excuses for not having already made the change may fall by the wayside.

Logistical Barriers

This final category comprises all of those "I can't because" barriers that have to do with the largely tangible responsibilities we have near our current homes or current situations.

- I can't because I have to take care of my aging mother.
- I can't because my child has special needs.
- I can't because my company will fall apart without my physical presence.

Some of these barriers can be the challenging to overcome, and it may take some difficult decisions and leaps of faith to get past them. Regarding the examples above:

You may have to decide how long you are willing to put your desires on hold to take care of an ailing loved one. This is deeply personal.

You may have to find a location or a series of locations that can provide the services you require for your child with special needs. There are children in other countries with these needs too. There will be work involved. It is a matter of deciding for you and your family where the cost / benefit line lies.

You may need to put a team in place that you trust enough to allow yourself to let go of the reins. Remote connection and periodic visits work well for many business owners around the world, including many that I have personally met in my travels and at home.

My point about this last category of barriers is simple: is it worth it to you? How badly do you want to travel, to live abroad or to make a change to your lifestyle? If you want it enough, you will find that solutions exist to almost all of the problems that fall into this category.

Do you have a logistical barrier that you feel you cannot move past? I would love to know about it and I promise to personally consider the situation and try to help you find a solution to it. Find out how to connect with me at the end of this book.

Whether the barriers for you are emotional, financial or logistical, almost all of them can be overcome with proper planning and sufficient motivation. As is often true, the cliché "where there's a will, there's a way" is fitting.

Building the Plan

He, who every morning plans the transactions of the day, and follows that plan, carries a thread that will guide him through a labyrinth of the most busy life.

Victor Hugo

This book is about living free of the boundaries of geography and the bonds of "the clock." By eliminating those restrictions, you can choose to live abroad, live at home or frankly live wherever you want, but it becomes *your* choice, and that freedom of choice is the absolute goal.

In Part 1, you began to define your goals. If they are not completely clear yet, that is normal. As you continue to read this book, perhaps they will become clearer. It may take much longer than that. Don't expect everything to fall into place overnight.

It is also important to realize that lifestyle design takes time, sometimes a few weeks, sometimes a few years. Enjoy the process and remind yourself regularly that while you are planning, your life is also happening. For this reason, I recommend that you not draw out your contemplation much longer than a few weeks.

Once your goals are established (or close to defined), you can begin to formulate your plan and transform them into your new reality. Planning may sound hard, but have faith in yourself and trust that the process will unfold well once you truly know what you want.

Pre-planning

Now that you have defined your ideal lifestyle, you need to figure out the obstacles on your projected path. As an example, I had identified the following as obstacles before we began our journey:

1. Maintaining education standards and French language development for my children
2. Mortgage on Canada home, and other financial responsibilities, such as car lease
3. Losing additional income stream and sense of accomplishment I get from work in Canada
4. Fear of missing family and friends

Make your list now and then continue reading. You may have more or fewer obstacles on your list. I am doing this from recall; I may have had other fears or identified other obstacles that have since vanished.

The obstacles that I will encounter when devising my plan:

1. _____

2. _____

3. _____

4. _____

Now it is time to take action.

Making the Plan

In this section we are going to figure out the small steps you need to take to get to your goal.

Lifestyle design depends on your action. **Now.** *Whether that means simply changing a thought process, starting to produce a plan* *or taking its first steps, without taking an initial action, you are not going to get anywhere new.* So, you are going to start today - not tomorrow, **today.**

In my experience, the first step is the most difficult. Committing to take action requires the most emotional energy. From there, once you get started, the momentum builds and you launch into your newly designed life.

In this section, you are going to make a concrete plan. This plan will have defined goals, objectives that relate to the goals, a timeline for achieving the objectives, and specific tasks that will help you to meet your objectives. Your plan is concrete, but it is also a living document, which means you can change it to respond to what is happening around you at any given moment.

Translating Goals into Objectives

By breaking down your goals into measurable objectives, you can assess your progress along the way. Let's revisit my goals from the previous chapter and see how I can translate them into measurable objectives.

My Goals

1. I want to be the one to accompany my kids to appointments, activities, school events.
2. I want to spend at least half the cold months of the winter where it is warm - Costa Rica is my second home these days.
3. I want to explore somewhere new a few times a year, separately with my kids, my girlfriends, and alone with my husband.

Objectives

1. Find work that allows me to be completely flexible. Work must be task-oriented and not based on the number of hours a day that I work. It must be online if I want to be able to work from anywhere.
2. Find renters for our house for the time we want to be away. We are not ready to sell it.
3. Transfer our car lease (i.e. have someone assume it).
4. Find a place to live in Costa Rica that does not require more than a six-month lease, yet costs less than our monthly expenses in Canada.
5. Use the difference between Canadian living expenses and Costa Rican living expenses to plan mini holidays within Costa Rica or elsewhere.

Try to break down your goals into objectives now that are clearly and easily measurable. For example, if I say, "find a place that costs less than my place in Canada," I can know for sure if I achieved this. If I say, "Do something about the car," I can't measure this objective effectively because "something" is too ambiguous.

Your Objectives

1. _____

2. _____

3. _____

4. _____

5. _____

6. _____

Costing Your Objectives

Right now you may be thinking that my head is in the clouds. *Find a job online that makes me enough income, move, then rent out my house? That is easier said than done, especially that first one,* you think. Well, yes and no. I will explore finding online work in more detail in the next chapter, but for now let's examine what it means to make "enough income" to follow your dreams.

I'm going to use fictitious numbers in this example because my mother told me it was tacky to talk about personal finances, and I always listen to my mom. The method described below is true, however, and is what we use to periodically assess where we are.

Example

- Live in Costa Rica in a well-appointed, furnished home with a minimum of two bedrooms and two bathrooms, air conditioning, and less than a five-minute walk to the beach - $1,000 to $1,500 per month.
- Cost of Canadian home including mortgage, property tax, and homeowner's insurance - $2,600 per month.

That's a savings of $1,100 per month. Yes, we live in a smaller place, but we live on the Pacific Ocean and are just as comfortable as we were in Canada, actually more so.

So now, look at your after-tax income and figure out how much less per month you can earn just based on the savings in rent alone.

Just wait until we go further into the costs of living in a later chapter -- the savings add up. This is completely doable; stay with me. Let's move on to how to create tasks from your objectives and in the next chapter we will delve into the hardcore "we're doing this!" steps.

Breaking Down the Objectives into Tasks

Some of the following example objectives are straightforward but still require further detailing. Others are more complex. The first objective — finding a flexible online job that is still fulfilling and pays the bills — is likely the most difficult and time-consuming. The others are just a matter of going through the required steps. I will deal with the work issue in the next chapter. In this one, let's look at the mechanics of dividing an objective into a list of tasks.

Example

Objective: Finding renters for your current home

Tasks:

1. Determine the rental market value of your home by asking two or three real estate agents to visit and to provide an evaluation. This service is free.

2. Do your own research on the current rental market. In our experience, rental agents get paid one month of the rental they obtain for you, so a hundred dollars more or less a month is not motivation for them, but it may be for you as it adds up over the long term. Therefore, aim high at first. We got $300 more a month than the agent suggested and we found a renter through friends, so we didn't have to pay an agent the equivalent of the first month's rent in commission.

3. Determine whether you need to fully cover the costs or if you just want to cover some of the costs and have someone trustworthy looking after your home. This may be worthwhile, especially if you are leaving for less than a year and your home is in an area where it is hard to find a

renter. We did this on our first six-month trip to Costa Rica. A friend of a friend was going through a divorce and needed a place to stay while she looked for a new home. She paid us about two-thirds of our costs, but as a single person put little wear and tear on the home.

4. Find out where renters look for housing in your community. Consider visiting professors, business executives, diplomats, etc. These types of people usually make the best renters, though there are exceptions. Do not rent to groups of students or young people in a group of roommates. These relationships among the renters are more likely to fall apart and jeopardize the lease agreement, and there also is more likelihood that your home will become a "party house."

5. List your rental on Craigslist, Kijiji and other free or inexpensive online marketplaces used in your community.

6. Post your offer on Facebook, Twitter and any other social media platform you use. Tell everyone you know or meet in person. Word of mouth worked for us both times we rented our home.

7. Hire a real estate agent if you are pressed for time or simply don't feel like doing the legwork yourself. This is perfectly acceptable, though it will cost you a month's rent and may garner less income (see point 2 above).

8. De-clutter. By getting rid of stuff, you are not only making your home more appealing to renters, you are also starting the process of feeling less bound to one place.

9. Check references and do a credit check if necessary. To be honest, I always check references, but rarely check credit.

10. Sign a lease.

11. Decide whether you will sell everything, put furniture in storage, or rent your home as furnished. We rented our home furnished and had the renters agree that we could keep our boxes of personal possessions in the basement storage room.

12. Pack! You are on your way.

There you go. One objective that is a small part of one goal is broken down into nine actionable, measurable steps that make it simple. While the number of steps may look daunting, the actions are straightforward.

Now you have enough information to help you formulate your own task lists to arrive at your goal. I want to make it even easier for you: if your goals are similar to mine (and they may well be if you're reading this book), you can use the easy-to-follow lists of tasks in subsequent chapters and the checklists in the appendix.

Part 3: Putting the Wheels in Motion

Don't look back. You're not going that way.

Unknown

Your dream is no longer a dream; it's a plan. You have attached a timeline to it and have measurable objectives. Now it's time to start working towards those objectives, and ultimately your goals.

This is where you start to feel like things are moving as you begin to check off boxes on your to-do lists. You can see exactly how you will achieve your goal, and with each action you take, you are a little bit closer to your new reality.

Streamlining Life

Less is more.

Robert Browning

In order to gain the freedom that our lifestyle affords, you must first get rid of "stuff," which can be material possessions, but also processes and habits that serve no purpose and clutter up your time. It also means getting rid of paper. I cannot tell you how freeing it is to receive almost no paper mail. It is so much easier to pop open an email and go directly to online banking payment than it is to open an envelope, discard the inserts, read the bill, file the bill, and pay the bill at some point in the future when you are at your computer.

Clearing the Clutter

Divest yourself of as many physical possessions as possible. Anything that you do not use on a regular basis should go. We kept one or two keepsakes from each period of the kids' young lives - literally, one or two. We also kept old family photos, albums, and a few pieces of silver from my grandmother. Everything else that wasn't mounted on the wall or used within the past couple of months was fair game.

For us, this meant that boxes of books and baby toys went to Goodwill. Big garbage bags full of our clothes went to the consignment store or were donated. Bags and boxes of receipts from the early 2000s were thrown away.

We sold anything and everything we didn't want online. We used Facebook resale groups, Craigslist, and Kijiji as our marketplace. Derek sold his electric guitar on eBay. We sold our 10-year-old Big Green Egg on Kijiji. A local consignment store took a bunch of decorative vases and bowls that were wedding gifts. They had not seen the light of day in the first 10 years of our marriage; I could not think of any reason why they would in the next 10.

In the two months that we spent clearing out the clutter, we made more than $3,000 selling various items. That covered our flights and first month's rent in Costa Rica, with funds to spare.

During our final weeks in Canada, we had a garage sale. It was not particularly successful; we were left with a ton of stuff to discard or donate and made little money.

Where should you sell, donate or discard your unnecessary items? *Note that I didn't call them "unwanted." You may want them, but that doesn't mean you need them or should keep them.*

Where to Sell Your Excess Goods

Online

- **eBay.com:** This can be effective for name-brand, sought-after goods. Generic items are hard to sell here. Remember to factor in shipping when you set your pricing.
- **Craigslist.com:** Find your local site, i.e., Ottawa.craigslist.com
- **Kijiji.com:** Find your local site, i.e., Ottawa.kijiji.ca
- **Facebook groups:** I found a local group for babies, toddlers, and preschoolers that was perfect for selling all the items my kids had grown out of. Search the target market you are trying to sell to in the Facebook search bar and request access to the group from the administrator. For instance, if you are trying to sell sheet music in San

Francisco, search "music teachers in San Francisco" or "music San Francisco" and see what you can find. In a big city, it may be useful to find an even more local target for more popular items; enter a neighborhood name as your search term.

Offline

- **Kids consignment shops:** Most towns, even smaller ones, have consignment shops for kids that take clothing, toys, books and other children's items that are in very good condition. Because kids grow and pass through developmental stages quickly, these stores are popular. Search online or ask around to find out which are the busiest stores in your town. I recommend using an established, reputable store because you don't want it to go out of business while holding your merchandise. Often these stores will ask whether you wish to be called if the item doesn't sell within their timeframe or if you prefer to donate to the store's charity of choice. Unless the item is particularly valuable, I recommend checking the "donate" box and knowing that you have one less item on your to-do list.

- **Adult clothing consignment shops:** This was the least successful of the shops for me because they often want in-season, on-trend, name brand clothing. I sold my best name brand clothing online through kijiji instead of sharing the profits with the consignment store. The few more expensive designer pieces that I own are classic and I wanted to keep them. What was left to sell was store brand clothing that was more worn or unique pieces from small, relatively unknown designers. Neither of these items would sell well in a consignment shop. I made about $150 from the sale of a few pairs of jeans and a blouse or two.

- **Houseware consignment shops:** This type of consignment shop was new to me. I had driven by the one near my home for 10 years before I set foot in it. I was able to sell many items, from unused scented candles to decorative pottery bowls, in this shop.

How to Donate Your Excess Goods

This should theoretically be easy, but here are two tips:

1. Find a service that picks up your donations on a specific day. This saves you a step. In Canada, the Canadian Diabetes Association provides this option. In the United States, many charities do this, so ask around or do an online search for "household goods donation."

2. Don't donate your garbage. If you have stained or torn clothing that you don't want or toys with missing pieces, recycle them or throw them away. Donate only items that are in good condition.

Now you have way less stuff and a little more cash, but you aren't done yet. It's now time to get rid of the paper.

Going Paperless

In order to ensure that we could live anywhere we wanted, we began the process of eliminating all paper mail. We already received several of our bills online, had a few set up for automatic payment, and whenever we thought of it, we asked to receive statements or notices by email rather than snail mail. Yet, we still received 3-10 pieces of mail per day in our mailbox. We needed to get more serious about this, so here's what we did, and you can do it too:

- **Bank statements:** Call your bank, either via telephone banking or a call to your personal banker if you have one, and ask that all your statements be e-statements. You may be directed to their online banking system. That's fine; at least you will be directed to exactly the right place in the system. This may save you several minutes, if not more. Make sure to choose this option for each of your accounts and any credit cards issued by the same bank.

- **Utility bills:** If you are moving abroad, you may eventually not receive these, but in the meantime sign up for online billing systems and set up automatic monthly payment. I recommend payment by credit card so you don't have to worry about cash flow within your bank account. Some utilities will only accept direct withdrawal. If so, just note on your calendar the day the payment comes out and give yourself a reminder three days before then with the approximate amount. This will allow you time to check your balance and transfer funds, if required.

- **Remote mail service:** You can get most of your bills and notices by email these days, but the government still likes the old-fashioned way. The Canadian government does not use email and will only mail out tax-related documents. My research indicates that the same is true of the United States government. This means that you need to retain a physical mailing address if you are retaining residency. We use a Canadian service called eSnail.ca. It is mediocre at best, but the only one we could find when we left Canada. It charges about $20 a month to receive, scan and email encrypted PDFs of our physical mail to us. The speed at which we receive the emails is inconsistent, which is why I am not over the moon about the service. So far, we haven't had any major issues, though, and for a small extra charge it will forward any mail that we need. We have done this twice for new credit cards at $4.

In the United States, several similar services are available:

- Virtualpostmail.com
- Mailboxforwarding.com
- Getmyusmail.com

- **Credit card bills:** Sign up for automatic withdrawal of the full balance (you are paying the full balance, aren't you?) from your bank account. Make yourself a note and set a reminder a few days before to ensure you have funds in the right account.

- **Dropbox or other online document storage service:** Sign up for an online document storage service that allows you to access your data from anywhere on any device. We use a couple, but started with dropbox.com. We store copies of every official document we have been issued. Guidebooks recommend travelling with paper copies of your passport in case it gets lost or stolen. My copies always end up lost or damaged beyond recognition from packing and unpacking. By having an electronic copy that you can access anywhere by simply typing in keywords from the properly labeled document title, you avoid this potential disaster.

We store copies of our passports, birth certificates, marriage certificate, immunization records, driver's licenses and frequent flyer numbers. You may also want to create a document that contains your credit card numbers and expiry dates and your ATM card number. I lost my ATM card and needed the number for access to online banking. I was able to get it through a Skype call with my personal banker's assistant, but it may not be that simple for you.

- **A trusted friend or family member as virtual assistant:** We receive most payments from our clients in electronic form, but there are always certain ones that can pay only by check. Rather than turn down that business, enlist a trusted friend or family member to be your occasional virtual assistant. My mom does this for us. We provide her address, and by email (or if the piece of mail is unfamiliar, during a Skype video chat), she describes the mail, opens it, and either files it or takes it to the bank to deposit it for us. Over the course of a year, she has done this four or five times. Be sure to thank this person when you see them next with a nice souvenir or a good bottle of wine.

Begin going paperless immediately. It can take months for some organizations to transfer you over to their electronic system. In a single month you may not receive bills or information from all your mailers. I would estimate it was three months before we were free of important paper mail. It is almost impossible to get rid of all of the flyers and junk mail directed to you or to your household. Simply accept this and place a recycle bin near your mailbox. When you leave, it will no longer be your concern.

Perfecting Your Processes

By clearing clutter and going paperless, you have already come a long way in streamlining the processes that help manage your life. In this section, we will look at additional tips and tricks that will make life simpler, whether at home or on the road. This includes tasks touched on above such as banking and paying bills, but we will look at more general ideas for making sure everything runs as smoothly as possible.

Decision-Making

You can't make decisions based on fear and the possibility of what might happen.

Michelle Obama

Your dream is no longer a dream; it's a plan. You have solidified the plan with a timeline and measurable objectives. Now it's time to start working towards those objectives, and ultimately your goals.

This is where you start to feel like this is really happening. You begin to check off boxes on your to-do lists. You can see exactly how you will achieve your goal, and with each action you take, you are a little bit closer to your new reality.

You have less stuff. You are now organized and mobile. It's now time to get on your merry way. You must figure out how to handle your home and any other assets in your current location, and you must plan for transportation to your destination, transportation at your destination, and living arrangements in your new home.

We arrived at this point in our own journey for the first time in February 2011. Having organized our lives so that we could live anywhere, we began planning our first extended vacation in Costa Rica. We would spend two months there. That was it.

As we began to connect the dots, book our airline tickets and organize schooling for the kids, we realized that two months was not going to be long enough. Here are a few of the reasons why:

- We could not rent out our home for two months, meaning we would be paying for housing in two places.
- If we wanted to travel within the country, we would be taking time away from school, for which we would be paying a full two months tuition.
- Two months would likely still feel like a vacation and we wanted to get a taste of real life.

We decided that we would extend our stay by four months and make it almost a full six months. The stage was set. We would leave the day after Christmas and be back in Canada the last week of June.

So, what went into the above decision-making?

- Choosing our destination
- Determining a time frame
- Choosing an educational plan for our kids
- Booking air travel
- Finding accommodation in a temporary home
  And what big items would we still have to check off our list?
- Finding a renter for our home in Canada
- Figuring out what to do with our leased car
- Figuring out daily personal transportation at our new location

These are just the big pieces of the puzzle. We will get to the smaller, more detailed pieces in a later chapter. First, we need to break down the decision-making process that we followed.

Choosing a Destination

Wherever you go, go with all your heart.

Confucius

While this book is not specifically about living abroad with a family - it can truly be about simply having the capability and freedom to live abroad - many of you are reading this book because you want to know how you can make travel or life abroad possible for your family. For this reason, I am dedicating the next few sections specifically to this topic.

Choosing Your Destination

We chose Costa Rica because we fell in love with the country and its people on our honeymoon. We then explored the possibility of living there with children and found that it suited our needs.

When you are evaluating a destination, consider your wants and then assess it based on your needs. Most people have a destination or a few potential spots in mind when they think about this type of adventure. This short list may have come from a childhood story, a vacation, or any other romantic, theoretical notion or experience.

From this initial list, evaluate your and your family's wants. What suits you and what do you want to get out of the experience?

- Are you hoping to develop new language skills?
- Are you hoping to experience a different climate, maybe escaping winter?
- Is a complete cultural immersion experience your dream?
- Do you simply want a change of scenery?

Note your wants here:

1._____

2. _____

3. _____

4. _____

You may or may not have gained some clarity; perhaps you have narrowed down your prospective destinations already. Write them down.

Our dream destination(s) is/are:

Now that you are clear about what you *want*, you are going to have to look at what your family *needs*. This may mean that you have to go back and revise your destination, but that is part of this process. So, let's look at your family's needs. Some considerations may include housing, education, transportation, communication, and access to healthcare.

Some of the many questions to ask yourself:

- Are modern conveniences important to you?
- Will you homeschool or do you want to find a school with a curriculum similar to that of your home country?
- Is language learning important?
- How important is it for you to be close to a hospital?
- Is a low cost of living important?

Take note of your family's needs here:

1._____

2. _____

3. _____

4. _____

5. _____

The next step is you doing your homework. This is critical to having a good experience abroad. Evaluate your needs against your wants for each of your dream destinations. Use the Internet to find out about each of your priorities and take notes. Eliminate places that are just not going to work for your family. This step will take time, but you will be glad that you did a thorough job.

A Cautionary Tale

My friend Nancy and I were having our regular Monday morning smoothie at a cafe in Tamarindo. We were talking about our usual subjects: kids, school, weekend plans and other mom chat. There was a family sitting next to us, a husband a wife and two young children around 2 and 4 years of age.

About 15 minutes after they sat down, the woman got up and came over to our table. "I am so sorry to interrupt," she said. "I just overheard your conversation and wanted to ask you what it's like living in this area."

Nancy and I chatted with her a few minutes, telling her about the different schooling options in the area, family life and town life. She told us that they were on their way to Nicaragua for their quarterly visa renewal -- Without residency, tourists must leave Costa Rica every 90 days to renew their tourist visas -- and had been on the road for five hours already that day, with a couple of hours or more to go.

They had moved to an area of Costa Rica that is hard to access because of the quality of the roads. She told us of her dream to, in her words, "live off the land" and enjoy a simpler life. However, that simpler life was complicated by their inability to access the rest of the country and its goods and services. She told us that she also felt isolated. There were other young families, but it was not what she had hoped. They were now contemplating a move to a more populated zone.

This is just one of many stories I have heard over the past couple of years. Many people have romantic notions about what they want for their family but discover that the dream was just that -- a dream. They had failed to evaluate their dream against their wants, and more importantly, their needs.

Had the woman in the story above considered her need for community, the requirement to travel eight hours each way every three months for visa renewal, and the fact that goods and services could be more difficult to access given their location, she may have found that her dream destination was impractical and would have saved herself the time, stress and expense of another move.

Practical is not sexy or romantic, but boy is practicality important when you are already outside of your comfort zone! It's precisely why we chose our destination.

Why We Chose Our Destination

We chose Tamarindo, Costa Rica, initially because of its beautiful beach and its language schools. Many other places in Costa Rica have equally (or more) gorgeous beaches, but Tamarindo has all the amenities and modern conveniences that make life in a tiny developing Central American country comfortable.

We have access to excellent local healthcare and a good quality hospital within an hour's drive. We have a choice of several schools that offer a variety of educational philosophies. We have enough restaurants and coffee shops within walking distance to keep Derek and me entertained. The town has relatively reliable Internet access to keep us working and connected. It has a lively community of young families.

Where in the World Will You Go?

Look back at your dream destination, your wants and your needs. Evaluate the destinations critically. You can make it work, but how hard are you making it for yourself? If it appears there are too many mountains to climb to get to that destination, consider another similar one where you can check more boxes off both your wants and needs lists.

In this chapter we looked at destination and I told you to do your research online. Where do you go to do that research? We will answer that question in the next chapter.

Using the Internet to Prepare

The more that you read, the more things you will know. The more that you learn, the more places you'll go.

Dr. Seuss

Thanks to the Internet, the world is truly a global village. You can stay connected with family and friends all over the world, speaking to them as if they were right next door, and develop business relationships with people around the world.

I have several clients in Australia. If I wake up to a simple assignment from them in my inbox, in some cases I can have it ready for them when they open their email the next morning. Time zones sometimes make us look great!

The Internet also provides an infinite number of research tools. We found housing in Costa Rica through a listing on VRBO.com. The hardest part of using the Internet for research is the volume of information available and the difficulty of verifying that information. Enter social media.

Social Media

With the proliferation of social media, not only are you able to connect with friends of friends all over the world, you are able to verify information, get second opinions and receive personal referrals about various services no matter how near or far from your home.

Here is how you can use social media, using Facebook as an example because it is the most commonly used:

- You can ask your friends for connections with their friends in distant locations
    - E.g., Status Update: I'm thinking of heading to Holland for a year abroad with my family next year. Does anyone have connections there who might be willing to answer a few questions?
- You can join groups that are forums of discussion about particular topics that may be of interest
    - E.g., Facebook groups such as *Expats in Nicaragua*; simply type it in the search box and ask to join.
- You can source housing, household items, cars and more in Facebook groups
    - E.g., Facebook groups such as Potrero Garage Sale or Tamarindo Rentals and Real Estate
- You can learn a lot about local businesses and the community by "liking" business Facebook pages.

I cannot stress how valuable social media is when you are abroad. It helps you stay connected to your community at home and helps you connect much more rapidly with your new community. You can stay "in the know" about local events and make personal connections that otherwise might be much more difficult and slow to achieve.

A Personal Research Visit / Vacation

Once you have narrowed down your destination possibilities to one, maybe two, or if you just can't decide, a maximum of three spots, you are going to start booking airline tickets. I strongly advise visiting any potential destinations before you make a final decision about spending a year there.

We had visited Tamarindo, Costa Rica, on three increasingly long vacations before we decided to spend six months there. You may be in a similar situation. You may have decided on a particular destination based on a wonderful experience you had on vacation. If this is the case, my strong counsel to visit would be softened, but I would still recommend doing in-depth research from abroad about what "real life" is like at that destination. Real life is very different from a holiday.

You must research all the components you will need to make life work for you for a longer stretch of time, such as daily transportation, grocery shopping, childcare, schooling, banking, health care (including dental care and mental health), security, and anything else you need for daily life at home that you will not be able to live without for a long stretch of time. You cannot assume that any essential option will be available at your destination; it may very well not be.

The good news is that you can find out about most of this online, via connections made through social media. I cannot emphasize enough that these mechanics of everyday life can be researched online, but you cannot assess the culture or intangible "feel" of a place without visiting in person.

The (strong) suggestion to visit may help you whittle down your list of potential destinations because plane tickets and your time spent visiting are not cheap. That's actually good news, because anything that can help in your decision-making process is welcome.

It's so hot here

I responded to a posting on the *Tamarindo Garage Sale* Facebook page. A woman was selling, among other things, a laundry drying rack – a strangely impossible item to purchase in Guanacaste. She invited me to come to her place to check it out and noted that I might be interested in other items that she had not posted.

I arrived at her place in one of the more upscale condo buildings in the area. A woman in her early sixties and a little dog greeted me at the door. The rack was perfect. I would take it. I spent a few minutes perusing the items on her dining room table. It was completely covered in grocery items and other household products.

As is my natural curious nature, I started asking questions. Why was she moving and where was she going?

Her story is not an unusual one, but nevertheless it and others like it blow my mind every time.

Three months before, this woman, her asthmatic husband and their little dog had sold their belongings and moved to the hottest province of Costa Rica. They had brought with them suitcases full of all their American comfort items including the laundry drying rack, a particular kind of Crest toothpaste, and what looked like a huge assortment of small kitchen appliances.

Her husband had already gone back to the United States. She was now selling everything and getting on a plane back to the U.S. because her husband found Costa Rica too **HOT**.

The expense, the time, the energy, the stress on their marriage could all have been avoided if this couple had just taken a four-day exploratory vacation prior to making the move.

Don't let this happen to you, especially with children in tow. Do your due diligence.

Putting Information into Context

Expats currently living in your destination of choice will almost always be open to sharing information with you about their experience. Some will share more than others and some will be more candid than others. All of them are sharing a personal experience filtered through the lens of their personal and cultural history.

Consider each insight from those on the ground in the context of your own family. Add it to your research as one part of a greater body of knowledge, but one story about one experience should *not* tip the balance in your decision-making process.

Taking Online Connections Offline

Over the years I have met several people online through friends of friends or social media and they have asked specific questions or had common interests. They were predominantly other travelers or expats looking for information or connection in Costa Rica, and some of them have become good friends.

Online connections can be an excellent source of comfort and stability in a new place. As the new arrival or visitor, it will be up to you to take that step. Invite your online connection for an offline coffee. He or she likely helped you with your preparatory research. Thank them in person, and perhaps a friendship will be born.

Have No Expectations

Just because someone answered questions for you online does not mean that they want to be your friend. Long-time expats have seen people come and go, and many have a hard time investing in new friendships if they believe that person may not be there for the long haul. Watching friends come and go can be emotionally draining.

This is not true for everyone, but be cognizant of this possibility.

Get Out of Your Comfort Zone

When you finally do arrive at your destination, I would urge you to get out of your comfort zone. Introduce yourself to people in situations where you might not at home. Use your children as talking points or even conversation starters. The more connected you are in your new destination, the more comfortable you will be and the more quickly you will feel "at home."

Ideas for making connections at your destination:

- Contact everyone you have corresponded with and invite them out individually to have coffee or a drink.
- If your children are in school, email the other parents and invite them to get together, with "class community" as your excuse.

Generally, in expat communities, a lot of newcomers are looking for connections, whether they arrived three months or three years ago. They will, for the most part, be open to having a chat.

Finding Housing

Home is where the heart is.

Pliny the Elder

There are two parts to this chapter and some that follow: a home country component and a new destination component.

In this chapter, we tackle what you can do with your housing in your home country and how you can put a roof over your head at your destination.

What Happens to Your Existing Home?

Many moving parts animate the discussion of what to do with your existing home. In this section I will discuss several scenarios with which most people can identify. There are going to be exceptions and tweaks needed to the suggestions, but you will have a good starting point for your planning.

One big question looms that you need to ask before you read any further: When (or if) you return to your home country, do you want to move back into the home where you currently reside? If the answer is "no", your next steps are simple.

- If you own: put your house on the market. Choose to contact a real estate agent or sell it yourself using one of the many FSBO (for sale by owner) marketplaces and tools, but don't wait. The sooner you have this taken care of and the money from the sale in your hands, the sooner you will feel the freedom that comes from unwanted material ties.

- If you rent: give notice to your landlord or put the date that notice is due on your calendar in red ink (or the electronic equivalent).

If you do want to move back into your current home when you return and you rent, the process may be slightly more complex.

1. Contact your landlord and inform him or her of your plans. Explain that you would like to sublet your home for the duration of your absence. Being especially complimentary of his or her property and management will go a long way toward making this possible. Give the landlord post-dated cheques if that is how you make payment each month. If you pay electronically, assure the landlord that you will be regularly available online and can easily send your payments from wherever you are.

2. Announce via social media and email to all contacts that you are looking for a tenant to sublet your home for the duration of your absence.

3. Place advertisements on commonly used free local marketplaces such as Craigslist.org and Kijiji.com and find even more localized sites that are targeted to your community, if possible. Ask around offline and search online for "rentals [YOUR TOWN NAME]."

If you own your home, you only need to worry about steps two and three above. Tell everyone you know and anyone you come into contact with that you are looking for a tenant. Announce it to your networks and ask your friends to share in their networks.

Place advertisements on free listing services and contact one or more real estate agents about listing the property, if necessary.

We found renters twice through word of mouth. The first time, we were leaving for only six months. Our postman actually found us a renter. He moonlighted as a real estate agent and had a client in the midst of a divorce. She had not yet found the property of her dreams to purchase, but she was eager to get out of her living situation.

In this case, because it was a shorter-term rental and we were thrilled to have a single woman as a tenant (less wear and tear on the house), we charged her significantly below-market rent.

In 2013, we considered listing the year-long rental with a real estate agent and spoke to a few about the market rate, but it was a friend of an acquaintance (contacted via social media) who rented it for full market value.

As we prepare to return to Costa Rica for the 2014-2015 school year, we are no longer attached to our home and are listing it with a real estate agent as "For Rent" or "For Sale."

Our time spent in Costa Rica has taught us that we can live with much less, including less physical space. Our home in Canada feels too big for us now, the extra space redundant and echoing. If it rents rather than sells this time, we plan to put it back on the market for sale after the lease with the new tenants expires.

TIP: Because our ultimate plan is a sale, the real estate agent has waived her commission on any rental based on a good faith agreement that we will list with her in the future. Consider asking your agent if they would agree to this arrangement.

To Rent Furnished or Unfurnished

So far, we have rented our home as furnished, which meant that we did not have to pack up much or find storage for our belongings. We gave some valuables to my parents, but the rest was left or boxed up and placed in a specified area in our basement. We find that the wear and tear is less of a problem than the hassle we avoid by having to pack and store more.

It is important to know that wear and tear does happen. Renters do not take care of your house as you would, no matter how conscientious they are. Both sets of tenants have broken and replaced items in our home. We have a set of dining room chairs currently under discussion, with different points of view on whether the damaged leather on each seat is from normal use or abuse. Be prepared for this. If you have irreplaceable items or items with sentimental value, do NOT leave them in the house.

You may feel that the hassle of packing is worth it because you cannot stomach someone living on your furniture. In this case, you will need to find a quality moving and storage company. If you have furniture and artwork that is irreplaceable, and you probably do if you don't want to rent your home as furnished, find climate-controlled storage. Mold, mildew and temperature extremes will damage it otherwise.

From Personal Experience

- I have found Craigslist.org more effective for finding tenants that Kijiji.com, though I have found the latter a better marketplace for selling goods.
- I have found 90 days the longest lead-time that people give themselves to find housing.
- Word of mouth can often be the most effective tool for renting your home. That is how we found renters on the two occasions.
- Real estate agents may be able to help you rent out your property. Commissions for their services range from a half to a full month's rent.

How Do We Find a Place to Live at Our Destination?

Whoa! Slow down for a moment and consider what you are looking for exactly. Have you defined that yet? If not, it will be hard to research, much less to describe to the people on the ground who are going to be instrumental in finding what you want.

You must define where you want to live:

- Town or village – could be a couple in the same area. For instance, you could live in a couple of towns around a school. You would define this to someone by giving them the name of the school and specifying the driving radius by time.

- Specific features of a neighborhood. Do you want to be within a five-minute walk to the beach? Is it important that you live in a walkable area or are you willing to get in your car for a quart of milk?

- What amenities are on your need and want lists for the property? A pool? An elevator? Parking? Do you need a detached home or would an apartment work for your family?

- What can you live with and without in the home? How many bedrooms? Which conveniences are essential?

For this last bullet point my list is small but inflexible. I need a dishwasher, an Internet hook-up and a clothes washer and dryer. During the rainy season nothing ever gets dry without a clothes dryer.

Your list might be longer or shorter. As long as you are clear when you start, you will have a better chance at getting what you want.

What if something on your list isn't available at your destination? That is okay. You will be able to rethink your priorities based on the list you started and the options available to you. You might compromise on a couple of amenities, or perhaps you have to reconsider your destination. Like the woman in chapter nine who had a dream of "living off the land," your dream of living deep in the jungle with all the comforts of home might not be feasible. Perhaps you can adjust your destination within the same country to get most of your wants while still filling the needs you have for housing.

A Note about Comfort

You are taking your family out of its comfort zone. While you may want to have as authentic an experience and as much cultural immersion as possible, remember that just living and interacting in a new place on a daily basis is discomfiting for even the most adventurous family. Romantic notions aside, consider each member of your family and their tolerance for change when you decide on how deep into cultural immersion you want to go.

Where to Look for a Rental

In the last chapter we talked about social media and online research. This is where you are going to put that research to good use. You should now have narrowed down your destinations to a couple of areas.

- Join real estate-related groups on Facebook in each of those areas.
- Ask for personal referrals from any and all online or offline connections.
- Visit vacation rental sites like VRBO.com, Flipkey.com and TripAdvisor.com. You may find property owners who normally do short-term rentals who may be interested in a long-term renter. We had success with this.

- Contact real estate agents in the area and check out the long-term rentals section on their websites. Most have at least some long-term rentals available.

Do You Need to Check Out the Property Before You Rent?

If you have never been to the area and you have no idea where exactly the property is located, I highly recommend visiting before you commit to a lease.

Our experience has been mixed. We BOUGHT our first long-term accommodation sight unseen and lucked out.

On our second long-term stay in Costa Rica, we decided to rent a larger apartment further from the beach so we could keep the property we owned as a vacation rental investment.

We rented a large 3-bedroom condo that looked good from a video tour. We had my brother-in-law, who was in Tamarindo at the time, give us a tour on Skype. It looked fine, not perfect, but definitely fine.

When we arrived, we felt the same way. Within two months we felt very differently. There was no storage, so we were constantly scrambling for storage solutions, and it had four bathrooms for its three bedrooms, one of which was always leaking, overflowing or smelling like a sewer after a heavy rainfall.

We complained repeatedly to the responsive property management company, but they were handcuffed by what the owner of the condo was willing to do. In this case, fixes only were approved, no replacements. So, we broke the lease and moved out, citing unlivable conditions.

We then moved to a place that I inspected with a fine-tooth comb.

That brings us to the legalities of renting property.

Get a Sense of the Law around Renting Property at Your Destination

In Costa Rica, the written law on leases and how it is applied are completely different. For example, leases are by default three years, though many are written for shorter periods. If your landlord tries to evict you before three years time, you have grounds to stay. In reality, this would be impractical, because you wouldn't want to live somewhere owned by an antagonistic landlord.

Ask at least a few people about the local laws and customs. One opinion is not necessarily an expert one. If you have any doubts, consult a local real estate lawyer to be sure.

In our case above, I asked a lawyer before we decided to move. She agreed that we were *likely* in the right, so we paid all of our bills, minus the security deposit, and left at the end of the last paid month. We were taking the risk that our landlord would take us to court, but we knew it wasn't likely because he lived in the United States and it would be more trouble than it was worth. We documented the problems just in case he did pursue legal action.

It wasn't a perfect scenario. It would have been ideal to find a dream spot on our first try. It was a learning experience and an exercise in the Costa Rican mantra of *Pura Vida* ("Pure Life"), more aptly translated in this case to *go with the flow* and also used as *life is good*.

We found our second rental through a real estate agent acquaintance. It was a nice condo in a gated community.

It worked for awhile but we felt isolated behind the gates. Getting to the beach required a drive or a 25-minute walk. The kids' friends were not nearby.

We stayed there for six months, but after the high tourist season was over, we moved into the vacation condo we owned by the beach.

Once there, we remembered what drew us to this country: daily walks on the beach, kids playing in the waves at sunset with friends, and an easy, slow pace of life. This was our place.

As you can discern from our story, no situation is perfect. It is important to match your wants and needs with your goals. Distill your priorities down to the very essence of your purpose abroad and you may hit your housing target more quickly than we did.

At the time of this writing, we are still living in our condo by the beach and loving it. In order to make it more affordable, we plan to travel over the December holiday period and Easter break period when we can pull in terrific rental income from tourists.

For the Truly Adventurous

If you don't mind living out of bags for a few days and have easy, flexible kids, you can always look for housing when you arrive, especially at low tourist season when those who own vacation rentals are feeling the financial pinch.

A good friend did this recently with her two sons. She arrived, and after one false start, found a fabulous condo for a reasonable price for as long as she was going to be there.

This is not my style. I like to know I have a place to land. It just depends on how much risk and uncertainty you can tolerate.

From Low to High, You Choose the Budget

When you are selecting a destination, you will be faced with a range of housing options at many price points. For example, we live in the most expensive tourist area in the country, but there are still places to rent for under $300 USD per month. You can also find large family homes for $2500-3500 USD per month or palatial estates for upwards of $10,000 USD per month.

The location, amenities and finishings of a house or condo are what determine the price. You must decide what you will accept, but options certainly exist for those with a tight budget.

A Final Note

It is important to avoid placing the expectations you have about housing in your home country, or about anything for that matter, on your life abroad. We don't live the same way we do in Canada as we do in Costa Rica. I tolerate the odd creature in my home, be they geckos, mini crabs or ants, though I do everything I can to get rid of the latter.

We understand that at random moments we won't have electricity, and at other times the water will be cut for a few hours. These shutdowns happen and we accept them because they are part of life in Central America, though we would be much less accepting of them in our home in Canada.

Deciding on Education

There are two things we should give our children: one is roots and the other is wings.

Hodding Carter

Whenever I tell people that I meet that we are from Canada and we live in Costa Rica, the questions begin. One assumption asked in the form of a question almost always arises. Sometimes it is posed as:

So you homeschool?

Other times the question is asked as:

How do you stay on top of the Canadian curriculum?

I can tell you with great certainty that I do not, and will not – I won't say "never, ever" because I don't want to jinx myself – ever homeschool my children. That decision was not made because I think there is anything wrong with the quality of education that homeschooled children receive, quite the contrary. I simply do not have the patience or temperament to do formal schooling with the kids, all day, every day.

That said, I must explain that we do a lot of natural teaching and innate learning in our home. I have a Bachelor of Education and it's hard for me not to want to take advantage of those teachable moments that arise so often on our adventures and in everyday life.

But we don't homeschool. We selected our destination because of the schooling options available to expats who are not residents of Costa Rica.

Beyond simply the private versus public versus homeschool decision, several other educational philosophies might interest you on your journey. Some private schools are based on particular alternative methods such as Waldorf or Montessori.

Or, you may not wish to embrace formal school at all. On our travels, we have met families who homeschool "a bit," unschool or world school.

What is unschooling? The unschooling, or worldschooling movement as it is sometimes called, is based on the teachings of John Holt (1923–1985). It is a branch of homeschooling that promotes unstructured, child-led learning with no set curriculum or schedule, as long as the child is happy and engaged. The philosophy is based on the principle that learning happens as a side effect of living a life with passion and exploring personal interests.

For more information on unschooling, visit unschooling.com, among many other websites dedicated to this practice.

The purpose of this book is not to explain the tenets or pros and cons of any one method of education. However, if you are open to new ideas or perhaps already going down a particular path, this may be the perfect time to explore more options.

Consider Education as a Factor as You Choose Your Destination

Non-resident children are not allowed to go to public school in Costa Rica, but in the Guanacaste province options abound for expat children, from United States-centric schools with some Spanish curriculum to fully bilingual and immersive.

All the schools have local students, whether they are from mixed expat-local parents or families simply looking for what the school offers as an alternative to local public education.

Within 15-20 km of our home are six private schools that might be or have been a good fit for our family. Clearly, educational options were a factor when we chose our destination.

Visit Potential Schools

On our second trip to Costa Rica we visited the one preschool/kindergarten that existed at that time in the area. Our kids were young and we did not know what our timeline looked like.

As time went on, the area became more populated and more schools opened. Some closed quickly, while others gained traction and a strong community.

On your research trip, book visits to any schools that look appealing to you from your preliminary online research. If that is not possible or you do not have time for the research trip, visit schools when you arrive before you make a decision.

Private Schools are Businesses

As Canadians who are primarily accustomed to the public school system, we learned quickly that private schools are businesses. A school may have a flashy website and the director or principal may speak in perfect harmony with your educational philosophy over the phone, but it could be that he or she is simply a slick salesperson who says all the right things.

I strongly recommend a visit to get a feel for a place before you commit to anything. Do not send a deposit, or worse yet, an entire semester or year's tuition without first seeing the school for yourself.

In the case of Central America, private schools/businesses operate in less-than-stable economic conditions and there are many stories of schools shutting down overnight and parents losing the tuition they had paid, as well as scrambling to find a place for their children to finish the school year.

Personal Referral

Ask your connections online and on the ground for personal referrals, personal experience AND hearsay or rumor about schools. While I would not recommend putting too much stock in a rumor, if it is consistent with other referrals or accounts you are hearing, that should be a sign.

Different schools work for different families for different reasons. Consider your needs and each of your children's needs before making a decision. Remember that your children will already have been thrown into a new community and culture, and therefore they need a soft place to land each day.

What Happens with School If or When We Go Back to Our Hometown?

Where I am from, Ontario, children are organized into grades by age group. This means I do not have to worry about my children being held back, but this wouldn't be a concern anyway. I picked a school in Costa Rica that I knew was equivalent to or (probably) better than our school in Canada in terms of getting the kids through the curriculum.

To reassure myself, from time to time I check on the Ontario government website to make sure they appear to meet most of the curriculum criteria. Much of the time, they are well ahead.

In some places, children will have to take a test when they register for school when they return to their homeland. If you select a good school in your new destination and pay attention to what your children are learning, they should be just fine. In fact, they should be better than fine.

The Benefits of Travel and Living Abroad for Education

Your kids are not preventing you from making a change.

In fact, it's not in spite of your kids that you are going to make that change, it is FOR your kids that you are going to do it.

"YES!" I thought to myself. It is <u>for</u> my children that we are living every moment of every day on our own terms. We are giving them opportunities and experiences that we hope they will cherish throughout their lifetimes.

Five Reasons for You to Travel with Your Kids

1. Kids who travel improve their educational performance AND future success.

<u>New research</u> has found that those who travelled internationally in their youth make $5,000 more annually and are significantly more likely to graduate from university than those who did not.

2. Increased cultural understanding in an increasingly globalized world.

If you have never observed other cultures in their place of origin, it is easy to misunderstand them. Traveling or living in places with different religious ideas, different customs, traditions and even simply different food can change one's perspective. It can make your kids more tolerant, open and less afraid of encountering situations and people that are different from their norm.

3. Increased gratitude

Children who experience other ways of life may appreciate their own situation more. I have a vivid recollection of sitting with my boys, then ages 4 and 6, at an outdoor restaurant in Granada, Nicaragua, when a little girl approached our table. She could not have been more than 3 years old. She asked if she could finish the leftovers on the boys' plates. When they nodded, she proceeded to hungrily wolf down the food, scooping big handfuls of rice and plantains into her mouth with her fingers. About four scoops into it, her older brother approached the table and scolded her for eating our food, reminding her that she should have known better.

Watching a street child hungrily gobble down the leftovers off your plate in a restaurant makes it easy to define poverty to a 6-year old and can stimulate a more complex discussion on inequality and fairness.

4. Living abroad increases the odds your child will become bilingual or multilingual

Research from the University of Manchester shows that kids who learn more than one language are better at planning and cognitive control, and have better working memories. In fact, it has also been shown that a child's ability to learn a new language is improved with every new one they speak. But the benefits don't stop there. There is emerging evidence that a bilingual childhood can delay the onset of dementia in old age by an average of four years.

5. Living abroad and traveling with your kids increases familial bonds

This reason is purely based on anecdotal evidence from our family and other families that we have met along our journey. When we travel together and live abroad, we are a team. Our support systems are fewer so we rely more on each other. We bond over shared new experiences, stressful situations, and steps outside of our individual comfort zones. In our case, the boys are brothers and best friends, now more than ever.

> Move about the globe with your family! New ideas and adventures await you and you'll make family memories to last a lifetime.

Considering Healthcare Options

Good health is not something we can buy. However, it can be an extremely valuable savings account.

Anne Wilson Schaef

Our health and the healthcare system were a factor in the selection of our destination. I wanted to know that quality services would be available to us should any of us need medical care.

As Canadians born and raised with universal health care, we have expectations about care that most countries cannot meet. When you are planning on living abroad, the destination must meet your healthcare needs, expectations and comfort level.

I was pleased to find that Costa Rica has one of the best healthcare systems in Latin America. It also has a public / private hybrid system, which meant we could receive care quickly if we needed it and were insured.

As in Canada, if you are visiting Costa Rica and are uninsured, you will be treated and stabilized, but you will have to pay for anything beyond that.

If you are insured, you can visit a private facility and be treated better than I ever was in Canada. That doesn't mean I haven't received excellent healthcare in Canada from superb, highly trained physicians, but in Costa Rica the private facilities are beautiful, clean, and affordable, and the staff are personable and well trained, in addition to providing top-notch healthcare.

Like most Canadians, the idea of a two-tier health care system makes me uncomfortable, but far from home, I readily admit that I appreciated the level of comfort it provided.

Expat Health Insurance

We purchased expat health insurance for our family. This particular policy covers us for expenses incurred in Costa Rica and anywhere else in the world, including Canada. Its only geographical limitation is two consecutive weeks of coverage in the United States.

Like most insurance policies, you can choose your deductible amount and the price of the policy varies based on your risk profile.

The medical and drug coverage for our family of four with no deductible was about $4,500 USD for the year. We were reimbursed about $2,000 USD for visits for each of us throughout the year for inevitable infections and illnesses, a couple of minor surgeries for Derek (don't ask...) and routine medications that we take for various pesky but non-life-threatening medical conditions.

After the first year, routine physicals are also covered under the policy.

Derek and I both feel that the $2,500 that was not reimbursed is a fair price to pay for the peace of mind we had over the course of the year. We knew that should anything serious have happened, we were covered financially.

For us, purchasing an insurance policy was probably an easier sell than for others accustomed to having their employers cover their healthcare insurance, or for Canadians or Europeans covered by universal healthcare.

We are self-employed and therefore have always purchased extended health insurance for charges that are not covered by the basic policy for all Ontarians, such as medications, physical therapy and similar treatments, and all kinds of other important services. Making this purchase was already in our annual plan, the cost was just higher this time.

If You Are a Gambler, Pay As You Go

On the flip side of the argument, I know that more than half of my expat friends pay as they go. When they need to see a doctor they make an appointment and pay the fee. There is nothing wrong with this approach either. This year, we would have come out ahead using this method. Again, we paid for peace of mind.

If you are curious about how much certain services cost in Costa Rica, here are a few examples:

- Routine family physician visit for minor health concern: $40-50 USD
- Lab culture: $40-50 USD
- Specialist consult: $90-100 USD
- Private ambulance with morphine drip to closest hospital (i.e., for broken bone or worse; the roads are so bumpy you need the drugs): $500 USD

They will call him "The Boy Who Fell off a Cliff"

My best friend brought her two children to visit us at spring break. Her son, a fiery redhead named Sam, was ready to have the time of his life. The day after their arrival, we took them to a restaurant with a pool and some table games high up in the hills overlooking the Pacific. It was common that on Sundays, after basketball practice, several families would gather together at a beach or pool for some downtime. The kids play. The adults chat. We all eat. You get the idea.

This particular Sunday started out no different. It wasn't unusual for one family or another to bring visiting guests. Sam immediately blended in with the group. He was sitting with a mom and a few boys watching others play Ping Pong. Sometimes the ball would roll through a barrier that separated the play area from the steep, gravel- and rock-covered incline that leads to the road which winds up to the restaurant. Usually one of the older boys in bare feet would carefully climb over the barrier and retrieve the ball.

That was, until the time Sam jumped up before anyone could stop him, and in his flip-flopped feet attempted to retrieve the ball. He got the ball all right, but continued to tumble head over feet 30 feet (10 M) down to the road below.

Sam's mom and I were not watching Sam. She was with her daughter at the playground and I was chatting with other parents by the pool. No one expects a kid of his age to hop over a barrier, and other parents were in the vicinity.

We learned that Sam had "fallen off a cliff" from my then 8-year-old. We pictured him sitting on the barrier and dropping through the air to land, SPLAT, on the ground below.

Panic ensued. We were in bare feet and tried to run to find him, but we could not walk on the ground because it was so hot. We ran in circles like chickens trying to find our shoes.

By that time, we learned that Sam was walking up the hill with an older boy who had run down the slope in his bare feet. Sam was bruised, scraped and covered in blood from his hairline to the tips of his toes. We laid him down on a table – every restaurant in Costa Rica has a massage table handy of course – and examined him to make sure nothing looked so serious that we shouldn't move him.

He appeared to have a broken nose, scrapes covering his body, including his fingers and toes from trying to stop his slide, and a sore wrist, but it was mobile.

In Costa Rica, at least in Guanacaste, you are told that 911 takes too long, so you are better off having a doctor's number in your cell phone and s/he can call a heli or regular ambulance, depending on your needs.

I called the doctor's cell. No answer. I called her office. No answer. After two minutes of debate, we decided to drive Sam to the closest clinic, but after calling there discovered the doctor had gone on a house call.

The phone rang. It was our doctor's fill-in calling. Our doctor was in the United States purchasing supplies for her new emergency clinic, but the fill-in could meet us at the clinic in 10 minutes. Off we went to meet her.

Sam was examined from head to toe by a wonderful nurse and a caring doctor. They cleaned his lacerations and he kept us laughing. His nose was so bruised and swollen, the doctor, nurse and we moms were certain it was broken. He would have to go to the Liberia clinic an hour away for an x-ray.

Sam kept complaining about his wrist, but the doctor performed range of motion and strength tests and determined that it was likely just sprained.

So, after paying the $100 bill for the emergency consult and medical supplies required to clean and bandage his wounds, three of us went to Liberia. We made a quick stop at our place to drop off the car and grab a taxi. I was in no mood to drive back late that night. The taxi to and from the Liberia clinic was $140.

The clinic was bright and shiny. We were greeted and ushered right into the triage area. A nurse asked us a few questions and a doctor then examined Sam.

The doctor ordered x-rays of Sam's nose and wrist. Sam's mom was called away to deal with her insurance. It turned out the clinic could seek reimbursement directly from the insurance company, so my friend would pay $0 out of pocket. While she was dealing with the finances, Sam and I were summoned from the exam room to the x-ray room. He was x-rayed, and as we later looked at the images together, his nose did not appear broken, but did the wrist seem to have a fracture? Why yes it did.

To be sure, the orthpaedic surgeon was called for the wrist and the plastic surgeon for the nose. Within 15 minutes we were deep in conversation with the plastic surgeon, who sported cowboy boots and tight designer jeans, about the softness of children's bones and the likelihood that the swelling was masking a break (not likely).

Then the orthopaedic guy arrived, slightly preppier but equally as well-styled as the plastic surgeon. He looked at us strangely when we burst out laughing as he announced Sam's wrist was indeed broken. We had been telling Sam it was fine and rolling our eyes at each other so much, that to be proven wrong was quite hilarious in that moment.

Sam's arm was casted and he was prescribed a variety of medications for swelling and infection-prevention, which we picked up at the pharmacy on-site. Finally, we were on our way back to the cab to take us home.

We were in Liberia for just over two hours, and during that time we saw the emergency doctor, dealt with the administration, picked up prescriptions, consulted with two specialists, and a cast was put on Sam's arm. *That* is service and efficiency.

What would we have done if Sam was in mortal danger after his fall? I don't think we would have been able to do anything differently. We would have called another couple of doctors, but likely would have had to take him ourselves to the new trauma unit 10 minutes away.

I have met a few individuals who vacation in Tamarindo but prefer to live near San Jose or Liberia so they can be close to a hospital. Those locations don't make sense for our family, so we absorb the risk.

I now carry the numbers of that new trauma center in my cell phone, as well as the numbers of two other doctors. By being further from a hospital, we are taking a calculated risk, of which I am acutely aware. However, as someone I know recently remarked, you are no safer or closer to medical care if you hike in the bush in Canada or ski on a quiet day in Colorado.

We take calculated risks every day, and for us the reward of living near the beach in a community like ours far outweighs its accompanying risk. Again, as in most of these decision points, you have to honestly evaluate your own level of comfort when it comes to proximity and access to medical services.

Deciding on Transportation

It is good to have an end to journey toward; but it is the journey that matters, in the end.

Ernest Hemingway

All kinds of transportation issues exist when you are planning life abroad or any type of mobile lifestyle. You must consider travel to and from your home country as well as everyday transportation. What kinds of factors should you consider, and which should influence your choice of destination?

I see four key components to travel and transportation for those living abroad:

- Making a plan for the vehicles you have at home
- Getting to and from your destination
- Getting around at your destination on a daily basis
- Travel at your destination; you are there, so you might as well explore, right?

What You Can Do with the Vehicles You Have at Home

If you have a vehicle or two or three at home, you need to plan to either divest yourself of it or have somewhere to keep it. The first time we left for Costa Rica, we had a vehicle that was only a year into its lease. We called the dealership to ask if they knew of a marketplace for subleases. The dealership said it would take the car back because the second-hand market for this car was hot. What luck!

When we arrived back from that six-month stay in Costa Rica, we leased another vehicle. Four months later we decided to go back to Central America. We tried to repeat the process with the dealership. This time we were not successful.

We tried LeaseBusters.com and would likely have found someone to whom we could transfer our lease, incurring only a small loss, but instead a friend decided to sublease from us.

That second time we learned: We do not plan on getting into any car leases in the near future.

If You Own Your Vehicle

- Sell it using the marketplace most commonly used in your area. These services range from free simple do-it-yourself sites to more costly full service operations.
- Store it with a friend or storage service.
- Lease it to a friend for the time you are away. The rules and legalities of this are specific to your province, state or country, so check with the appropriate authorities before pursuing this option.

Travel To and From Your Destination

This is a must. You will have, at minimum, a one-way trip to your destination. More than likely, you will also have a trip home from your destination. As you plan your new lifestyle, consider the cost and the quality of these trips.

Things to consider:

- What is the average cost of travel at various times of the year?

- How long and how many legs is the trip? Are the flights direct or do you have to change planes? Does that mean retrieving your luggage for customs?

- What about ground transportation at home and at your destination? How will you manage that?

The Cost of Travel

At peak times of the year, as in the dead of Canadian winter, the cost of travel to Costa Rica is more than double what it is in August or September. This is true for most tourist destinations, based on their high tourist seasons. Consider this in your planning.

You will also want to think about luggage restrictions. From my experience and that of most of my friends and acquaintances, shipping is expensive and thus not a good option. Smart packing should allow you to pay for only a bag or two extra on the airline, but be prepared. Understand the rules and restrictions so you are not surprised with extra charges at the airport.

For our family of four, we brought eight duffle bags that included new bedding and a whole lot of sports equipment. We will return from our destination with no more than six bags, leaving many of our clothes, shoes, baseball gloves and linens.

As far as linens go, we brought new sheets for the condo we own. Most condos that are rented as furnished will provide linens, but you may still want to bring your own.

How Complex is The Trip?

My husband is not a happy air traveler. The more he flies, the more comfortable he gets, but it is certainly not fun for him. For this reason, flight times and convenience are paramount for us.

We plan our trips based on routes, total travel time and overall comfort, in addition to affordability. Derek would much rather add a car or shuttle trip at the beginning or end of a trip, rather than have to take a second, or even worse, a third flight leg. This is especially true when we fly in winter, when storms often delay flights or ground them completely, making successful connections less likely.

Depending on how often you will be traveling to and from your destination, consider all that is involved in the voyage. Our trip to Tamarindo from Canada normally looks like this:

- Taxi or shuttle to airport – 15 minutes
- Flight to Toronto or connecting city in the Northeast U.S. – 1 hour
- Flight to Liberia, Costa Rica airport – approx. 5 hours
- Shuttle to Tamarindo condo – 1 hour

Our day usually consists of 12 hours of travel time from door to door. It's long, but acceptable to us.

This amount of travel may seem reasonable to you or it may be beyond your acceptable limits. Go with your gut instinct. What can you do comfortably with your family and your baggage?

For me, trying to journey to the Far East or Australia would be out of the question right now. If you are true to yourself and push yourself without stretching too far, you will find the sweet spot for your family's travel.

Ground Transportation

When booking your trip(s), do not overlook ground transportation requirements. How will you get to the airport at departure and then from the airport to your destination with all that luggage?

We use a shuttle service on both ends. We specify the amount of people and bags we will have, so the company is prepared and sends an appropriate vehicle; we also are quoted an accurate price in advance.

You can find shuttle services by searching online for the airport location with "shuttle" or "airport shuttle" as keywords. If you are concerned about reputation, check the companies out online on a site like TripAdvisor.com. Remember, one bad review is usually an exception, but many bad reviews are a red flag.

Other options for ground transportation include taxi, but this is risky if you have a lot of bags, or rental car. Again, you will need to make sure that there is enough space for your luggage and your family members. Unless you know the area quite well or your final destination is close to the airport, I would not recommend getting a rental car at the airport. It is just another task you have to contend with after a long journey.

Getting Around on a Daily Basis

When you have selected a destination, you will have considered the type of community you want, including whether or not it is a walkable or cycling community, a city with great public transportation, or a place where you will need your own car.

If you can walk or cycle to get most of your essentials, do that of course. If your city has good public transportation, use it! If you want to explore the region, rent a car only when necessary -- a huge savings of time, energy and hassle.

However, if you live in a community where you need a car more than three times a week (fewer than that and I would recommend taking cabs; it will be less expensive), you may want to find a long-term lease or purchase a car at your destination.

Where we are in Costa Rica, there is a high turnover of used vehicles with tourists and short-term residents coming and going. This drives the price higher for good second-hand vehicles, but it also means you can usually find something serviceable and be fairly certain you can resell it if and when you decide to return to your home country.

We found both a long-term lease and a used car to purchase by word of mouth after having asked everyone that we spoke to about our trip if they knew of anything available.

On our first trip, our property manager had a car that he leased to us for six months. On the second trip, it was the tenants who were vacating our apartment who sold us their car.

Renting a vehicle on a monthly basis from a rental car company is also an option, but it is definitely the most expensive of the three. Leasing or sub-leasing is less expensive but harder to find. Purchasing a car requires more cash upfront and the risk of repairs along the way, but once you sell you are more likely to come out ahead with this option. That's why we bought a car the second time around.

Insuring a Vehicle

Non-residents in most places have the right to own a vehicle and the same responsibility as residents to pay appropriate taxes, registration and licensing fees, as well as insurance fees required by the country or jurisdiction.

To find out what is required in your area, check with websites catering to expats of that region. Have a local lawyer assist you if you are unclear on the law. You can find a reputable lawyer by asking in Facebook groups dedicated to your region. Again, remember that one recommendation (or one bad review) is not sufficient to form an opinion, unless you know the referrer personally. Get a consensus before you trust an individual or a business.

Remember to consider the type of car that is appropriate for the conditions in your community. The car we leased was tiny and not ideal for the rugged terrain that exists in parts of Guanacaste province. It worked for us, but it meant that we got a ride or took a shuttle a couple of times rather than trying to navigate that little car around potholes and through creeks. This suited us because our comfort level in more remote areas was not great in the beginning.

Driving in a New Country

Traffic and safety laws vary from country to country and jurisdiction to jurisdiction. Be sure to learn what the laws are in your area before you drive. Know the written rules and do your best to discover the unwritten rules. Understand that some rules may be enforced while others won't be, and they may be enforced for some groups and not for others. As a guest in a foreign land, you cannot change these customs so you must learn to adjust to them.

In some countries, you will need to acquire a local driver's license after a time. In other places, they may require at least an international license from the day you arrive on their soil. Do your research.

The Booster Seat Paradox

Guanacaste is known for random roadblocks and traffic stops by two groups of officials, the *tráficos* (traffic police) and the *policía turística*, which translates to "tourist police" but really means immigration officials.

The *tráficos* are enforcing the rules of the road and the *policía turística* is looking for undocumented workers or expired tourist visas, essentially people who are in the country illegally.

The police randomly (or maybe not so randomly) stop cars. To date, I have been stopped twice but have passed through about two dozen roadblocks. The boys were with me on my second stop. At the time, Charlie, my 6-year-old, was in a booster seat. Dexter, my 8-year-old was not. The officer explained to me that Dexter had to be in a booster seat until he was 12 years old.

"Twelve!" I exclaimed as my inner gringo came out and I continued in my best español, "but in Canada, where the laws are so strict, kids only need to be in them until 8 years old."

Just then, a pick-up went by filled with a group of children in the bed of the truck. He looked at me expectantly as I watched the truck pass. In this country, kids can ride in the back of a pick-up truck, but they must be in booster seats until they are ready for their bar mitzvahs.

This law seemed so absurd that I was sure the police officer was making it up in an effort to extort money from what he thought to be a stupid tourist. "The ticket is $360," he said.

"Oh," I said, thinking myself smarter than this seemingly corrupt man of the law.

I waited. There was no way I was going to offer him $20, as most of my friends do when they are being threatened with a ticket. This guy was not going to pull the wool over my eyes.

"I'll make sure to put him in a booster seat from now on," I said, smugly daring him to write me a ticket.

Puzzled, the police officer waved me through.

A couple of months later I recounted the story to my friend and lawyer over drinks. She laughed and exclaimed, "Isn't that law silly? Nobody does that."

I was shocked. The law is REAL. In Costa Rica, the police will let kids ride in the back of a pick-up or on a scooter without a helmet, both of which I believe are technically against the law, but they will make a kid sit in a booster until they are almost adults.

That police officer must have thought me really naïve or really ballsy. Oh, and I never did get that second booster seat.

Planning for Wanderlust

You are in a new place. Your world has opened up. If you are like most, you will want to experience all of what your new destination has to offer, which often means regional travel. Plan for it.

While we spend far less on entertainment abroad than we do at home, our in-country travel expenses are more frequent and thus a larger line item in our budget.

Expect to travel more and do so. You have stepped outside of your everyday routine so that you can experience everything your new home has to offer. You do not want to look back at this time with any regrets.

The Real Budget

It's impossible to map out a route to your destination if you don't know where you're starting from.

Suze Orman

You may be wondering if you are not putting the cart before the horse if you look at housing, education, transportation, and healthcare before you establish your budget. In some ways this is true. However, you have to know what is available in a given area to determine if that area is for you. Once you know what you can realistically get in terms of quality of housing and education for a given price, you can create a more realistic budget.

Developing a Detailed Budget

In Chapter 6: Building the Plan, you may have already begun to create a budget. Now it's time to refine that budget based on the research you have done.

Take out the budget worksheet that you used in Chapter 6. If you wrote in pencil, find an eraser and start filling in the figures you discovered through your research. If you wrote in pen, print out or download the budget worksheet at familyfreedomproject.com and fill in the new, more accurate numbers.

Self-Reflection

Honesty with yourself and conservative planning will set you up for success when it comes to budgeting. Ask yourself: does the budget meet your needs and your expectations? Do you still think you will be saving money, living at par, or spending an amount of money per month from your savings with which you feel comfortable?

If the answer to the above question is "no," it is time to reflect on what can be cut back, or perhaps how you can increase the revenue side of the equation during your period abroad. If the cuts mean that you will not achieve the goals you have for your lifestyle, you may have to rethink the timing or the destination.

- Is this the right destination for you?
- Can you find something similar in a less expensive country or region of the same country?
- Is the timing right?
- Should you spend another year establishing your online business before you depart?
- Can you take a little more time to save before you depart, with the understanding that you will ultimately have less to compromise on afterwards?

These are hard questions. While I love to tell people to jump in with both feet, I would really hate to see anyone get less than the most out of an experience because they had to compromise on too much. Part of turning a dream into a plan and then a reality is ensuring that the plan is well crafted and thus the reality is just as you had hoped.

Costa Rica versus Canada: Cost of Living For our Family

In our estimation, in Costa Rica we spend 65% of what we spend on a monthly basis in Canada. Here are a few examples of interesting line item comparisons:

- Groceries, for us, are slightly less expensive, though not more than 10%. While local produce is less expensive, imported foods such as decent cheese, chocolate or breakfast cereal can be more than double.

  We have changed our diet to consume more local items, incorporating new fruits and vegetables, but that still leaves us almost even. People who shop only for organic and imported goods complain incessantly about the cost of groceries.

- Housing costs are about half, factoring in utilities and maintenance costs.

- We save about 20% on restaurant meals, and we enjoy eating out at least a few times a week. Restaurant meals are much fresher and more nutritious here, since there are fewer pre-packaged food wholesalers that serve restaurants.

- Our entertainment costs are less than 25% of those in Canada because we spend most of our time with friends at the beach. We are an hour away from the nearest movie theater and there is no bowling alley or indoor playground to woo our children.

- Speaking of the kids, their after-school activities are 50% less costly in Costa Rica. Qualified, skilled instructors for sports and arts charge rates that are in line with the local economy.

Charlie participated in a theatre program with a director who runs the same program in Canada in the off-season for three times the price. Sports programs are equally affordable.

- Communications cost run at about 25% of those that we pay in Canada. Our cell phones costs about $5 a month, and we do not have a landline. Cable is about a third to a half of what we pay in Canada.

- Clothing and shoe budgets are about 60% less in Costa Rica. Our uniforms consist of shorts or trunks, tees, flip flops and sporting gear for the boys and men; bikinis, ultracasual dresses, flip-flops and fitness/yoga wear for the girls and women. No costly winter coats, stylish boots or other gear are necessary.

- We find home maintenance and housekeeping is 75% less expensive in Costa Rica. For this price, many expats (us included) treat themselves to regular cleaning and housekeeping services.

If something is not working at home or in the car, repairs are much less expensive, unless you need a new part, which is often imported. Yet, the need for new parts seems to happen much less frequently. Since the parts are so expensive, mechanics and maintenance workers are more likely to fix something than replace it.

Online search, discussion, connections, self-reflection and a research trip are all important tools to help you create a realistic budget. Failing to plan properly sets you up for unmet expectations and disappointment. Proper planning will set you and your family up for an experience of a lifetime.

Part 4: Your New Reality

Courage is not the absence of fear but rather the judgment that something is more important than fear.

Ambrose Redmoon

You dreamed it. You planned it. Now it's time to start living it. This section is not critical to the execution of your plan, but it may provide some inspiration to help you take the final steps.

These are the myths, the stories and the questions that people just like you and me ask, tell and enjoy along the way. This is the fun part! Maybe your story will be part of the next edition.

Your Questions Answered

There is only one success – to be able to live your life in your own way.

Christopher Morley

I am a member of a couple of Facebook groups for expats in Costa Rica that are full of myths, stories, hearsay, misinformation and factoids mixed in with really useful, good quality information. These groups are a never-ending source of controversy and comedy.

Online, myths about living abroad abound. Make sure that you do your research using a reputable source to verify any information you find online.

Here are some of the most asked questions and the corresponding answers that I give to prospective expats moving to Costa Rica. Though this may not be your destination of choice, the type of questions to ask and even their answers may be of interest no matter where in the world you are heading.

1. How do you do your banking?

In Costa Rica, US dollars are accepted everywhere. We opened a US dollar account with our Canadian bank, and trade at a preferred rate that was arranged ahead of time with our bank. The more we trade at once, the better our rate. We then withdraw funds through a bank machine in US dollars.

As much as possible, we use a US dollar credit card issued by our Canadian bank for purchases. This allows us better track our spending and avoid those nasty cash withdrawal fees. However, many small businesses, when asked, will offer a worthwhile discount if you pay in cash because the fees charged to them by Visa and Mastercard are significant.

2. What do you do for healthcare while you are in Costa Rica?

We purchase an annual expatriate health insurance policy with no deductible that covers almost everything we need, at least it has until now. This means we usually pay for services out of pocket and are then reimbursed by the insurance company after we submit the receipts. The insurance company deposits the money onto our credit card in the currency of our choice, US dollars. They also offer direct deposit.

3. How do you handle immigration issues? Are you allowed to work legally?

We are halfway through the process of getting temporary residency as investors since we own property. On our first extended stay, we entered and exited on tourist visas that last for 90 days. These are issued as a stamp in your passport as you cross the border. To renew your visa after 90 days, you must leave the country for 72 hours. Many expats use this "border run" as an opportunity to explore bordering countries like Nicaragua and Panama.

We are not permitted to work in a Costa Rican business and do not qualify for a work permit as we are not yet residents.

4. Is it safe? Is their violent crime like in Mexico?

Many places in Latin America do have reputations for kidnappings, drug cartels, and associated violent crimes. Costa Rica does not. There is definitely theft and petty crime and we take precautions with our personal effects just as we would on vacation in any country where the locals perceive a significant difference in standard of living. We watch our stuff carefully at the beach, and we keep our wedding rings in a safe. Most buildings have security, and if they don't, they are vulnerable.

Certain areas of the country are more notorious for crime than others. So, like you would with any of your travels, look at each area and consider its history and tendencies.

5. Should we get immunizations? Are any mandatory?

Though I recommend that everyone make sure all of their immunizations are up to date for their own state or province, there are no mandatory immunizations to enter the country, but you will need to have an up-to-date immunization record for school. Non-residents are not required to have immunizations to attend school, at least in my experience.

I am not a doctor nor is this medical advice, but I also recommend asking your travel medicine specialist or family doctor about the following additional immunizations:

- Hepatitis A
- Hepatitis B if you are going to be working closely with others or if your child is at school or in daycare
- Typhoid, as a precaution for certain areas of the country

6. Can I drink the water in Costa Rica?

We love Costa Rica for this. Unlike Mexico and the Dominican Republic, Costa Rica's water system seems to agree with travelers from further north. We still purify our water using some sort of filter for taste and mineral content at home. However, we never hesitate to order tap water in restaurants or ask for ice in our beverages.

7. What do you do for phones?

Oh, how Canada can learn from Latin America when it comes to mobile phone service. We purchased inexpensive Nokia phones for about $35. We spend about $10 every two months on pay as you go service. This way, we can take our phones with us to the beach, on the go, wherever, and not be afraid to lose them. We do not have a landline, and keep one of our Canadian iPhones for wifi and a camera.

Many of our friends use their smartphones everywhere, but they are often breaking them, losing them, replacing them, and this is just too likely with klutzy us.

8. What does your family eat there?

Well, we are a difficult family when it comes to eating. I am a vegetarian who will occasionally eat sea creatures and the kids and Derek really dislike fish. So, we eat simple meals that can be customized to each family member's preference. This is the same, whether we are in Canada or Costa Rica.

In Costa Rica, we always have a pot of beans and a pot of rice in the fridge. These are our weekly staple. Derek eats these for lunch and we use them as the basis for one or two evening meals each week. Our fridge is also always full of chopped up tropical fruits like mango, pineapple, cantaloupe and watermelon, sliced carrots and baby tomatoes.

Our favourite evening meals are tacos, pasta, chicken breast and roasted potatoes, and burgers. Vegetables are almost always green beans, broccoli, cauliflower and/or carrots. Boring, I know. But that's what they eat!

Derek and I miss good, crisp lettuce. Salads are often lackluster unless made right before you eat them, which is tough at the hectic dinner hour. I found a great restaurant that makes my favourite salad for me at a reasonable price. That's my go to lunch.

9. Are there snakes and if so, are they poisonous?

Yes and yes. But I haven't seen any close up in the wild, only in a serpentarium. My friends have though. Better to expect it than to be surprised. Make noise. They are afraid.

10. How do you deal with the heat?

I just do. We all just do. If you don't like the heat, then Guanacaste is not the Costa Rican province for you. On most days, we move less in the middle of the day, while we enjoy the first few hours and the last few hours of the day outdoors.

My Expat Friends

Remember, Mondays are fine. It's your life that sucks.

Ricky Gervais

Get inspired by reading the stories of expat families with kids. I remember that day just over ten years ago when Derek and I watched that expat family playing with their children on Tamarindo Beach and how they inspired us.

Let these stories short interviews be your inspiration:

Nancy and Jacqueline

This was the first installment of a regular feature on the Family Freedom Project blog. Every couple of weeks I profile an expat family that has found their freedom.

My first ever interview was with my good friend Nancy. She and her daughter Jacqueline moved to Costa Rica after tragedy spurred Nancy to make a change. Here is our interview.

1. *I am so happy to have you share your life with us! Can you start with a little background on yourself and why you chose Costa Rica as your home?*

On July 30th, 2012 my boyfriend, John, passed away. It was 2 weeks before our daughter turned 4 years old. I spent the next year completely numb. I woke up every morning, took my daughter to school, and went to work. I rarely saw my daughter and knew that we needed a change. We needed to live and not just to exist.

We sold all of our possessions and moved to Tamarindo, Costa Rica almost a year to the date of John's passing. I chose Costa Rica because I had lived here from 1991-1993 and absolutely loved it. I knew it would be a great place for us. I chose Tamarindo because of the proximity to good schools, and international airport, and of course the beach!

2. ***From my experience moving to a new place has a 'fairy tale' quality on arrival. Was that the case for you and your family when you moved to Costa Rica?***

Not exactly. We had so many good friends and a great support system in Hawaii and I was nervous hoping that I made the right decision. Would Jacqueline like her new school? Would we make good friends? It took about 6 months to feel at home, but now I am sure we made the right decision.

3. ***Do you feel like you will live in Costa Rica forever? Will you go back to your native country or perhaps move on to somewhere new? Do you ever think about going back? Why or why not?***

We have no plans to leave Costa Rica although you never know what life holds. I can't think of anywhere else I would like to live at this point. The main reason we moved here is so that I wouldn't have to work for a while and could spend more time with Jacqueline. If we moved back to our home country of the United States, I would definitely have to go back to work. As for moving to another country, I can't imagine that we could replicate the serene, low stress life that we have here.

4. Can you explain how you handle residency and/or working in Costa Rica? What can you tell readers about supporting yourself in Costa Rica?

Once we arrived, we immediately applied for residency and are still in the process of obtaining it. We are living off of savings and eventually I will have to go back to work, but I plan on finding a job online so that I can work from home and set my own schedule. I am currently working on a memoir chronicling our life from John's death to our move so that is keeping me busy while Jacqueline is in school.

5. Can you compare family life in Costa Rica to family life where you are from? How do your kids like it? This is a hot topic for people looking to move abroad with families. Will the schools be good? Will they adapt?

For us, family life in Costa Rica is amazing. I never imagined that I could be able to spend so much time with my daughter. Tamarindo is a small town without even one traffic light so we don't spend a lot of time in the car running around like crazy. Although we lived in a small beach town in Hawaii, there was a lot of driving around to various activities and running errands.

There is also so much to do here. The weather is just about perfect everyday, so we spend a lot of time with friends at the beach. There are also a ton of outdoor activities that we enjoy. We have gone horseback riding, white water rafting, surfing, and enjoyed sunset catamaran tours.

Finding a good school for Jacqueline was a top priority. There are 6 international schools in our area and they are all very good. Aside from traditional education, the schools in Costa Rica really take advantage of the proximity to nature with gardening classes and tons of field trips. Also, I love the fact that Jacqueline is learning a second language.

Before we left and when we first arrived I worried about Jacqueline adapting, but kids are amazing at making friends and we have lots of play dates.

6. *What about healthcare? Is that a concern?*

I knew from living here earlier that Costa Rica has very good health care. We got a catastrophic policy that allows us to seek healthcare anywhere in the world and for routine doctor visits we just pay up front.

7. *What do you wish you did differently in planning?*

Actually, I am quite happy with the planning we did before we moved. I did a lot of research and flew down here for a week to tour schools and look at real estate. I thought long and hard about the decision before I put an offer on a condo and sold all of our things.

8. *Is there anything you wish you had brought with you that you don't have?*

Only small things. Since there is no Target or Walmart in the area, I wish I would have brought down more kitchen items, but every time I return to the States, I pick up a few things.

9. *How are your language skills? Does that make a difference to your life?*

Because I lived here before, I learned Spanish. For me, it does make a difference to be able to speak the language.

10. *Do you have anything more that you would like to share with my readers? They would love to hear your stories and your insights.*

I think that moving to another country with children is an amazing adventure. I have absolutely no regrets. I would advise people to make sure that they have budgeted properly, to not have cultural expectations from their home country, and to not expect everyday life to be similar to a vacation.

You can learn more about Nancy's memoir as it develops by following her Facebook page *Moving Forward: From Tragedy to Sunshine*, and check your local listings for her episode on House Hunters International.

Margaret and Odin

I met Margaret through our sons who are classmates. I would describe her as interesting and engaging, and thus I wanted to tell a little bit - the surface really- of her story. Margaret decided to live in Costa Rica for two reasons. Read the interview below to find out more:

1. ***I am so happy to have you share your life with us! Can you start with a little background on yourself and why you chose Costa Rica as your home?***

In August 2004, I was a production coordinator for a not-for-profit theater company in East Hampton, New York. I was working on a production for a benefit out on eastern Long Island at the time. One of the performers, a Martha Graham trained dancer, invited me to join him and his boyfriend on a trip to Costa Rica.

This was August and the trip was planned for October. I remember him saying Costa Rica is "so great" and at the time, flights were only $270 USD round trip.

I told him to book the ticket. I am not and have never been a planner, I just usually go with the flow and make plans same day (or a day or two) in advance.

But he booked the ticket.

The trip was only supposed to last 10 days. For a New Yorker, 10 days seemed like forever. How could I possibly leave for so long?

Before I knew it, October 10th arrived and off I was on my journey to Costa Rica. I didn't think much about where I was going. I knew only that it was a tiny country in Central America, though I never ever got it confused with Puerto Rico as many New Yorkers do. I also knew that many New Yorkers went to Costa Rica for winter vacation but all went to Tamarindo. My friends and I were headed to the raw, rare Caribbean side of Puerto Viejo, Talamanca.

It was important to me that we go somewhere completely off the beaten path. I had no desire to spend money to go to another country to see all the same people I knew from New York. Nixon, my friend, looked at me with assurance and said, "Trust me; this is worth it".

So off we went. And I met my son's father. The 10-day trip turned into 3 weeks.

2. *When and why did you make Costa Rica your home?*

My son was born in New York. Not long after, I decided that I could no longer take the cold weather of the East Coast nor did I want to practically deal with it. Things like changing my closet clothes from winter to summer, they all felt like such a waste of time.

Financially, I had no desire to pay for a heating bill or buy winter clothes. I wanted to wear the same clothes all year round. It was pretty organic; the things that were bothering me led me to where my son's father was.

That was important. I realized how much I wanted my son to know his natural father.

3. *Do you feel like you will live in Costa Rica forever? Will you go back to your native country or perhaps move on to somewhere new? Do you ever think about going back? Why or why not?*

I do not feel like I will live in Costa Rica the rest of my life, but I try to keep my head where my feet are and live one day at a time. Like I said in the first question, I have never been a planner.

4. *Can you explain how you handle residency and/or working in Costa Rica? What can you tell readers about supporting yourself in Costa Rica?*

Being a single mother, I have no idea what the day will bring regarding support, I just know the sun will always set and that's worth a million. I am a massage therapist licensed in NY State and I support us to the best of my ability using that mobile skill set.

I want to thank Margaret for sharing this part of her story with us here. I am hoping to unravel the rest of the story in book two of the Family Freedom Project. Hold your collective breath until then.

If you are in Tamarindo or surroundings and want a fabulous 5 star massage by a registered therapist, check out Margaret's Facebook page and get in touch. You will NOT regret it.

Kate and Family

Kate moved to Costa Rica from Nova Scotia, Canada and she is pregnant with her fourth child – in a few months she will be mom to 4 kids 5 years old and under. In our interview, Kate shares her feelings about the first few months in her new home.

1. *I am so happy to have you share your life with us! Can you start with a little background on yourself and why you chose Costa Rica as your home?*

I have both British and Canadian citizenship. I lived my first 17 years in the UK, and then moved to Canada. After I moved to Canada, I met my future husband and 10 years later, we have 3 busy little boys and baby #4 is due in October. When I met my husband he was in the

Canadian military and our life together began quickly with a posting to Nova Scotia, Canada.

Here's a quick synopsis of our last five years:

2009: First son born in Nova Scotia. Husband takes parental leave and begins an online business in marketing/advertising.

2011: Second son born in Ottawa which is next military posting. Business is still doing well.

2012: With business booming, husband retires from the military with 10 years of service.

FREEDOM!

2012: Pregnant and moving again. Drive across the country to Victoria, British Columbia on Canada's west coast.

2012: Sell home in Ottawa; Victoria is now home -briefly.

2013: Tired of throwing away $4000/month on rent; search for a home to buy. Start questioning this move. Victoria weather is good but cost-of-living is not. Offer to purchase a home in Nova Scotia that we find online, on condition of seeing it. Fly the whole family to see it. Buy it. Move ourselves and our furniture – AGAIN. Promise ourselves this is the last move.

January 2014: Coldest winter ever. One month in Mexico is not enough. We are miserable.

February 2014: Husband LOVES to extensively research things, and gives me a list of warm places that could meet our needs.

March 2014: Costa Rica is top of the list based on online research. One crazy week in March rent a home, register oldest two for school, and visit hospitals – pregnant again.

Every night on this trip we sit on the beach in Playa Grande and watch the sun set. It feels right, it feels like an amazing place to raise our children. The people are so friendly and the atmosphere is so laid back. We go home and put our house on the market expecting it to take a while to sell. Three days later our house is sold.

We leave Canada on May 30th.

2. From my experience moving to a new place has a 'fairy tale' quality on arrival. Was that the case for you and your family when you moved to Costa Rica?

I was terrified on arrival. I anticipated all the bad things. It would be too hot. The bugs would be bad. Someone will steal from me. I expected the worst.

I had moved from the UK to Canada; I knew that the first year in a new country would be hard, and reminded Chris about this all the time.

But moving here has been absolutely liberating. Maybe it's because I expected the worst, but everything has gone smoothly. I am enjoying learning about the area. Every day brings new challenges, but we conquer one challenge at a time and have developed a routine.

3. Do you feel like you will live in Costa Rica forever? Will you go back to your native country or perhaps move on to somewhere new? Do you ever think about going back? Why or why not?

I do feel like I will live here forever. When I left Canada I wanted a Plan B, in case Costa Rica didn't work out. Now that I am here, I cannot imagine moving back to Canada. Now that I am not there, I can see all the things about Canada that I don't miss. Things that are so different here, but in a good way.

- I don't miss pulling handfuls of junk mail from my mailbox every day.

- I don't miss my children being inside for most of the year.

- I don't miss commercialization aimed at my children.

- I don't miss the processed food that fills the supermarkets. (Editor's note: Costa Rican supermarkets are filled with processed food too, but they are much easier to avoid at the local outdoor markets!)

We are building a house here, and our short term plan is to stay for 5 years. "Forever" is a scary word, so we are taking it a few years at a time. My oldest child will be starting Kindergarten, so I would like my children to settle and make friends.

4. Can you explain how you handle residency and/or working in Costa Rica? What can you tell readers about supporting yourself in Costa Rica?

We are fortunate because my husband's business is doing well and he is able to work from home, anywhere in the world. So that gives us financial security without the stress of trying to find a job or start a new business.

When we moved here we knew that we wanted to do it properly. Running to the border every 3 months is not for us. We used an agency called Send Me South to help us with all the paperwork and they have been worth every penny. It's honestly been easy and stress free. We are here on a student visa which is valid for 1 year. After the year is up, we can renew it or roll it over to residency because in October our fourth child will be born in Costa Rica. Having a relative born here gives us residency.

5. Can you compare family life in Costa Rica to family life where you are from? How do your kids like it? This is a hot topic for people looking to move abroad with families. Will the schools be good? Will they adapt? etc...

We are a close family. I have been a stay-at-home mom for 5 years and Chris has worked from home for the last 2 years. This means we always do everything together. We are a strong family unit and have never had other family in close proximity. It doesn't matter where we are, as long as we have each other. This part hasn't changed much.

Living in Costa Rica, my children are outside all the time. My cautious 5 year old finally learned to swim and his 3 year old brother isn't far behind. There is so much to do and see here. Even a trip to the local fruit market is an adventure. My children love bagging up random fruit and taking them home to try. The kindness of strangers is absolutely amazing, and they all love my children.

I found a school online before we had even visited Costa Rica. After going there in person, and learning more about their mission and the children's daily activities, I am so excited for my children to start in September. I don't think I could have found a better school in Canada.

6. What about healthcare? Is that a concern?

When we visited in March we already knew I was pregnant and that I would possibly be having a baby here. Health care here is amazing! They have a public system and a private system.

I don't know much about the public system yet because I have only been going to a private hospital. The local clinic here has a bilingual doctor and they have specialists visit the area routinely. For example, this weekend they have a gynecologist, a nutritionist, a plastic surgeon, and a dermatologist taking appointments.

My obstetrician works at a private hospital an hour away, and that is where I plan on giving birth. I was nervous when I heard that Costa Rica has high C-section rates. I learned that this is because you can elect to have a C-section. To give birth naturally, the price is $3500 and for a C-section it's $4500.

After having two home births in Canada, a birth with medical intervention is the last thing I want. I looked into working with a midwife, but we decided to have the baby in hospital because of distance and the inconsistency of ambulance service in an emergency.

I have had two OB appointments and have paid cash because we don't have insurance. To me, the prices seem reasonable for the world class treatment with state of the art technology. For example, I paid just under $100 for a consultation including the extensive 20-week ultrasound and a 1-month supply of prenatal vitamins.

From my experience with the private system, for me, health care is better here than it is in Canada.

7. What do you wish you did differently in planning?

I wish I'd come sooner! So far, we are happy with all of our choices.

8. Is there anything you wish you brought with you that you don't have?

We flew first class so that we could bring a lot of luggage on the plane. We also bought my youngest his own ticket, even though he could have flown for free as he is under 2. We did this because in the end it was cheaper to buy pricier seats and have the extra perks of 2 checked bags per passenger. We checked 12 items and we carried on 6 or 7 items. And there was still more I wanted to bring!

All of our other possessions are in a shipping container in San Jose, being stored until our house is ready. We have more than we need and the only things I wish I had are silly little things:

I miss my slippers and I miss wearing pants. I wish I had brought my cat. And salt and vinegar chips....

9. How are your language skills? Does that make a difference to your life?

I came here knowing absolutely no Spanish. And now I know about 20 words, all the words that you need to be polite. It is not essential to know Spanish. A smile and a giggle are the same in every language.

It's important to me to learn the language. It's hard right now with so much else going on. But my goal is to take some Spanish classes – soon.

10. Do you have anything more that you would like to share with my readers? They would love to hear your stories and your insights.

There are a lot of people – friends, family, strangers – that don't understand our choices. That's ok. We do what we do for us. We don't let fear hold us back, and we believe that as long as we have each other we can do anything.

We have made mistakes (Victoria, BC feels like a mistake) but it's all experience. You cannot be afraid to fail.

My advice: Feel the fear and do it anyway.

We were living a life waiting for things to happen, waiting for Friday, waiting for summer. Now we live every day to its fullest, in a beautiful country full of endless adventure and possibility.

The follow up to Kate's story, including details about labour and delivery in Costa Rica, will be available in the next book.

Stephanie and Family

Stephanie and her family were just about to depart from Canada for a year of Spanish immersion in Costa Rica when we spoke in August of 2014. She describes her motivation, preparation and organization for the journey.

1. *I am so happy to have you share your dreams with us! Can you start with a little background about your family and describe your wish to relocate?*

We're a family of four (our kids are now 8 and 10 years old), and we live in a small 'village' in Quebec, Canada, just outside Ottawa. Our children's education until now has been completely in French, and they are bilingual as a result (English/French). However we also want them to start to learn Spanish, and want them to do so through an immersion experience within another culture.

2. *Do you want to move temporarily or permanently? Will you go back to your native country or perhaps move on to somewhere new? Why or why not?*

At this point we're moving temporarily, and plan to return to Canada after one year. Logistics, such as our current jobs, are the main factor in that plan. However we're open to the idea of extending our time away if it becomes feasible. This will also be influenced to a large extent by how things go during the year (with work and extended family members back home for example).

3. *Can you explain how you plan on handling immigration concerns and/or working in your new home? What can you tell readers about how you will support yourself at your destination?*

Regarding immigration concerns, we've chosen a destination that allows foreigners to remain in the country for extended periods, on the condition that they do exit periodically. That was part of our decision-making process. And it gives us an excuse to visit some neighboring countries :). In terms of supporting ourselves financially, my husband will continue to work remotely (he is self-employed and works online even when we're at home). I've taken a leave of absence from my job for a year, and have been saving money for a year and a half in anticipation of going away. It hasn't been easy, especially since we've been doing major home renovations in that time, but we've "pinched pennies" anywhere possible – I even put myself on a cash budget for a few months. But it's been worth it to have this upcoming adventure awaiting us!

4. Can you compare how you see family life abroad to family life where you are from? What are your plans for schooling your children?

While we're abroad, our children will attend a private international school (only local residents may attend the public schools where we're going). I anticipate that our family life abroad will be quite different. We will of course still have homework to do and school projects to complete, but I envision more quality family time - No 9-5 job, nor a long commute to work, and in general a feeling of wanting to make the most of this time away together.

5. What about healthcare? Is that a concern?

We're fortunate in that our home health care plan will continue to provide coverage for us while abroad. This is something worth exploring with your provincial plan (if you're in Canada), and depending on the reasons for your travel, you may be eligible for continued coverage. The healthcare situation is certainly something important for families to explore, to ensure that they're comfortable with their level of coverage while abroad, and to look into private insurance if necessary.

6. How have you found the planning process? What resources can you share with readers? What resources do you wish you had in your planning process so far?

The planning process is fun! The Internet has definitely been our #1 resource, and we've reached out to other families that we've found online who are doing something similar. It helps to run thoughts and questions past those who have already done this or are in the midst of their adventure. I've come across families relocating for a specific period, some who are travelling to different areas and homeschooling while they go, and others who are simply going with the flow and have no concrete plan or date to return home. People DO do this! There is also a Facebook site for "Families on the move". This is a closed group and I haven't actually joined it, but could be useful to some readers.

7. *How are your language skills? Do you plan to learn or will you try to get by on what you have now?*

We're headed to a Spanish destination, and my Spanish is rusty (it was once very good). I plan to take some classes at the outset to start working on it once again :). But I love the language and want to re-learn it, so that component is actually a bonus for me.

8. *Do you have anything more that you would like to share with my readers? They would love to hear your stories, ideas and your insights.'*

As mentioned above, I've found the Internet to be a great source of information, and an interesting way to come across other families doing similar things. When we were contemplating a European destination, I found a number of homeschooling families making their way across Europe, and some on to Asia. Their stories help to provide ideas for "must-see's and must-do's", and they usually provide contact info if you want to ask them further questions. For any readers contemplating the homeschooling-while-travelling option, there were certainly families online doing the same thing, and it would be worth reaching out to them. Also, we've been planning our trip for over a year. Certainly people can prepare and take off in a shorter time frame than that, but we've been gradually preparing for it. At the outset, I made a list of everything that had to get sorted out before we could go. This included both broad and specific things like:

- Request leave from work
- Formulate financial plan and budget
- Apply to school/determine schooling plan
- Purchase flights
- Sort out healthcare
- Immunizations if applicable
- Passports up to date
- Prepare house for renting and find tenants
- Find housing at our destination
- Cancel utilities, Internet etc
- Address Internet, phones etc at our destination
- Provide travel notification to the bank and credit card company

The list you make can seem a tad overwhelming, but it can be achieved. In our case, slowly but surely, those items started to get checked off the list, and with each one I felt like we were one step closer to going. **And now, the dream has made its way to reality!**

What are you waiting for?

Heard enough? Then go to it. Put your plan into action.

Not convinced yet, or perhaps you simply want more? Then read other stories like these, get tips and inspiration, and ask all the questions you want at FamilyFreedomProject.com.

Additional stories of expat families with kids will soon be available in the second Family Freedom Project book. Sign up here to be notified of its release and to be kept up-to-date on important Family Freedom Project news and information.

Appendix

Find all sorts of useful tools and stories for your new lifestyle at FamilyFreedomProject.com including:

- <u>Moving Abroad Checklist</u>
- <u>Monthly Budget Comparison Planner</u>
- <u>Travel Packing Checklist</u>

About the Author

Liisa Vexler lives with her husband and two sons in Tamarindo, Costa Rica. A dreamer and a realist at the same time, Liisa has enjoyed a number of different careers over the course of her lifetime. She was a dancer on a Canadian Forces variety show in Bosnia, a medical researcher, an event planner, a Canadian Football League cheerleader, a medical writer, and most recently an author and speaker.

On their honeymoon, Liisa and her husband Derek fell in love with Costa Rica. They designed their lifestyles so it could eventually become their second home.

The Family Freedom Project is Liisa's first book.

Acknowledgements

A number of books provided useful information, most notably *The 4-Hour Workweek* by Timothy Ferriss.

I'd like to to thank my mom, Françoise for being my most trusted and honest reader, and my dad, Ron, for his unwavering support and concern. My gratitude also goes to my brother Dan who gave me a journal for my 29th birthday and told me I would write one day.

Thank you to my editor, Ralph Stice, for his shared passion for the topic and desire to make the book better. My proofreader Pete Laughton offered structural tips outside of the scope of what I asked which improved this guide.

A sincere thanks to Genna Robustelli of Tamarindo Family Photos for the cover image that captures the spirit of the book, as well as for the photo that accompanies the author biography. Rachaela Brisindi deserves kudos for creating a cover that pulls the pages together beautifully.

I am grateful to all those who asked questions and inspired this book. I am equally indebted to those who shared their families' stories so willingly for the Family Freedom Project blog, this book, and the upcoming anthology of expat family stories. Jim Parisi of Jaime Peligro Bookstore, was an invaluable sounding board throughout the process.

Thanks to my children, Dexter and Charlie, who have helped to shape our lifestyle and my "why". And of course, Derek, who is my harshest critic and most fervent supporter.

70548438R00075